T0391177

Rights Limitation in Digital Age

Shaojun Liu

Rights Limitation in Digital Age

Reform of Fair Use in Copyright Law

Intellectual Property Publishing House Co.,Ltd.

Shaojun Liu
Beijing Acadamy of Social Sciences
Beijing, China

Translated by
Shibao Wang
Intellectual Property Publishing House
Beijing, China

An Zhang
Intellectual Property Publishing House
Beijing, China

Hao Wang
Intellectual Property Publishing House
Beijing, China

Jie Wang
Intellectual Property Publishing House
Beijing, China

ISBN 978-981-16-4379-8   ISBN 978-981-16-4380-4   (eBook)
https://doi.org/10.1007/978-981-16-4380-4

Jointly published with Intellectual Property Publishing House
The print edition is not for sale in China (Mainland). Customers from China (Mainland) please order the print book from: Intellectual Property Publishing House.

Translation from the Chinese language edition: 权利限制与数字技术 by Shaojun Liu, et al., © IPPH 2019. Published by IPPH. All Rights Reserved.
© Intellectual Property Publishing House 2021
This work is subject to copyright. All rights are reserved by the Publishers, whether the whole or part of the material is concerned, specifically the rights of reprinting, reuse of illustrations, recitation, broadcasting, reproduction on microfilms or in any other physical way, and transmission or information storage and retrieval, electronic adaptation, computer software, or by similar or dissimilar methodology now known or hereafter developed.
The use of general descriptive names, registered names, trademarks, service marks, etc. in this publication does not imply, even in the absence of a specific statement, that such names are exempt from the relevant protective laws and regulations and therefore free for general use.
The publishers, the authors, and the editors are safe to assume that the advice and information in this book are believed to be true and accurate at the date of publication. Neither the publishers nor the authors or the editors give a warranty, express or implied, with respect to the material contained herein or for any errors or omissions that may have been made. The publishers remain neutral with regard to jurisdictional claims in published maps and institutional affiliations.

This Springer imprint is published by the registered company Springer Nature Singapore Pte Ltd.
The registered company address is: 152 Beach Road, #21-01/04 Gateway East, Singapore 189721, Singapore

Preface

From the perspective of the world civilization history, changes in social relations along with the significant development of technology are usually manifested by legal system reforms. The scientific and technological revolutions are the important driving force for the emergence and development of the modern intellectual property system, which is a system of rules gradually formed with the development of modern industry and market economy. Moreover, in modern societies, technology development determines the rise and fall of industries and the changes in market practice. Inevitably, this will in turn exert great influence on the intellectual property system. Such influence is mutual, meaning that the new technology not only presents new problems and challenges to the existing intellectual property system but also provides novel ways to solve the problems and respond to the challenges. The interaction between the technological development and that of the intellectual property system is a long-term, cyclical process; legislators must consider, under a new technological circumstance, how to protect the interests of creators and other rights holders, promote the dissemination of works and information, and popularize knowledge, thereby improving the well-being of the society as a whole.

The system of limitation on copyright is a system that balances and mediates the interests of the creators and the public. In the Internet era where the application of digital technology is ubiquitous, new types of information technology are emerging, enabling people to overcome the traditional time and space constraints on obtaining information and thus disequilibrating the interests between rights holders and users in the traditional copyright system. The system of limitation on copyright mainly includes two types, namely *fair use* and *statutory license*, wherein the fair use system is the start point for reviewing the limitation system. The development and application of digital technology have brought about a new state of imbalance between the fair use of copyright and the right abuse of rights holders. The boundaries of fair use have been affected in some industries, and the interests of many rights holders are therefore seriously affected. In addition, new forms of works produced by integrating the new technology may, due to the dominant strength of the rights holders, discourage the public from being creative. At this point, more attention should be paid to the statutory license system as the endpoint for studying the system of limitation on copyright, and the balance of interests between the rights holders and the public should be readjusted accordingly.

The fair use system is not a statutory right of the user, but the statutory obligation of the rights holder. It is a necessary constraint on the scope to which the copyright owner can exercise his or her rights. The essence is that, within the scope of the rights of the owner, the copyright law grants an exemption for the specific acts that are recognized by the law and that are insufficient to cause any substantial injury to the copyright owners. In other words, the law does not consider such acts infringement. As be spoken in practice, this system is an institutional paradigm that guarantees the individual rights and makes the rights in harmony with the public interests; it not only effectively protects the copyright owners from infringement on their proper and substantive rights but also facilitates and promotes the public's proper and limited use and dissemination of literary, artistic, and scientific works.

In civil law jurisdictions, a system of limitation on rights mostly bases the copyright law on specific exceptions[1]; while the common law jurisdictions have developed and established a system of limitation on copyright, similar to that of the civil law countries, by case law based on the doctrine of fair use (such as "fair use" in the USA and "fair dealing" in the UK). The fair use system is, originally created by judges' judgments, an important means to protect against infringement of copyright. It is also one of the most important statutory restrictions on the excessive control of rights by rights holders. Therefore, the doctrine of fair use plays a positive role in free dissemination of works and the protection against the negative effects of excessive implementation of monopoly by copyright owners.[2]

Fair use owns a key role for maximizing the utilization of works from the perspective of limiting the interests of copyright owners. For a long time, as a part of the controversial system, some believe that the main roles of fair use can be reflected in the following aspects: first, from the economic perspective, the legislative cause of fair use is largely understood as a way to fix market failures[3]; second, it is conducive to promoting social values such as justice and democracy[4]; third, the

---

[1] For instance, Section 6 of the German Act on Copyright and Related Rights contains the "limitations on copyright," which specifies in an enumerative manner the limitations on and exceptions to copyright with regard to fair use and statutory license. This law also defines the user's obligations in different situations. The Italian copyright law lists the specific use behaviors in its "exceptions and limitations" and specifies the circumstances in which the rights holders' right to remuneration should be guaranteed in different activities. During the recent years, the Japanese copyright law has undergone many revisions and also paid attention to the continuous improvement of the limitation on the copyright system and has continuously added new right limitations to the regulations.

[2] Bunker M. D. Eroding Fair Use: The 'Transformative' Use Doctrine After Campbell [J]. Communication Law and Policy, 2002, 7 (1).

[3] Gordon W. J. Fair Use as Market Failure: A Structural and Economic Analysis of the Betamax Case and its Predecessors [J]. Colum. L. Rev., 1982, 82 (1600); Xiong Qi. On the Applicable Scope for the Fair Use System of Copyright [J]. Science Technology and Law, 2006 (2).

[4] Netanel N. W. Copyright and a Democratic Civil Society [J]. Yale L. J. 1996, 106 (283); Fisher W. W. Reconstructing the Fair Use Doctrine [J]. Harv. L. Rev. 1988, 101 (1659). Quoted from a quotation, Bunker M. D. Eroding Fair Use: The "Transformative" Use Doctrine After Campbell [J]. Communication Law and Policy, 2002, 7 (1).

Preface vii

conflicts between monopoly rights and freedom of speech can be balanced[5]; and fourth, it can provide people with practical ways for intellectual creations on the basis of their predecessors.[6]

For safeguarding the rights of the owners, when new technologies gradually eliminate market failures, the scope of fair use will inevitably narrow. Otherwise, it will cause losses to the rights holders. On the contrary, if theoretically fair use is considered to protect freedom of speech, the impact of new technologies on the scope of fair use will significantly be reduced; the scope could be expanded by limiting the copyright under the new technical conditions. The limitation on the scope of fair use application depends on the theoretical values of the legislators. The examination of the theoretical values comes from the consideration on the performance of the system. An important factor in judging the performance of the system is whether the ultimate outcome of legal practice is beneficial to the growth of social wealth that is not only reflected by the changes in the balance of economic interests, but the aspects of politics, culture, and life as well.

As the copyright system has always been subject to the technologies for creation and communication, the widely applied digital technology has a profound impact on all kinds of intellectual property including copyright to make the intellectual property system adjust or restructure. The flow of knowledge discussed in the modern society no longer focuses on communication or dissemination by means of roads, trade, and trade fairs. The copyright law has experienced three major leaps from printing technology, broadcasting, and television technology, to digital technology. History has proven that the reform and development of copyright law and the expansion and changes in copyright rights are all driven by economics and the investors' pursuit of economic interests in copyright-related industries. When new technologies reduce transaction costs and create new financial incentives, rights holders will mostly tend to expand their rights to a border scope to cover the newly created interests, such as the rights of performer, record producer, and broadcasting organization, and the rights for information dissemination via the Internet. Correspondingly, the traditional profit-making approach may gradually disappear due to the technological changes (e.g., e-book shave gradually replaced some of the printed books in the market). In the course of the above-mentioned systematic changes, any growth or decline in copyright will affect the copyright system to different degrees, among which, the most influential one is fair use.

The circulation of works is the way to realize the benefit of copyright but may be hindered by the high cost of licensing, which is referred to as a mode of "prisoner's dilemma"; it seems that the best way to solve the problem is fair use, but the development of new technology has greatly reduced the licensing cost, for example, the utilization statistics of works can be performed easily on a digital platform. In

---

[5] For instance, the conflicts between the US copyright law and freedom of speech emphasized in the First Amendment. Quoted from Lohmann F. V. "Fair use as innovation policy" [J]. Berkeley Technology Law Journal, 2008.

[6] Leval P. N. Toward a Fair Use Standard [J]. Harv. L. Rev., 1990, 103: 1105, 1109–1110. Quoted from Lohmann F. V. Fair use as innovation policy [J]. Berkeley Technology Law Journal, 2008.

the chain of interest, the copyright system centers on "author-communicator-user." The communicator has an increasingly prominent status and is in charge of the interests as a dominant role, especially in the Internet environment where the ability of network service providers is totally different from traditional publishers in nature and roles. Realizing and distributing benefits has become increasingly conspicuous. The traditional publisher plays a crucial role in selecting authors, publicizing works and the like to gain income. However, the network provider can not only replace the role of the traditional publishe but also provide the author and the user with a more free communication platform and allow the author and the user to have more freedom in transaction. Moreover, network provider can create an unprecedented market environment for the formation of the supply-demand chain for works and determine the value of the works. This in turn helps to bring new opportunities and challenges to the intellectual property trading market. However, this has also caused confusion that whether the fair use system still exists in a "fair and legal" way in the new market environment. In the past, the transaction cost method mainly analyzed the balance of interests between the rights holders and the users, which is a binary structure in economic analysis. Nowadays, the communicators in the circulation chain of works own growing interests and roles. Therefore, the analysis and judgment of the role of the communicator should be added into the study of fair use. In particular, the nature of private copying and the potential conflicts brought by it should be concerned under digital technology.

This book emphatically discusses the challenges of the change in the dissemination way of works brought by digital technology to the system of fair use of copyright and analyzes the so-called fairness by the study of theories on the system of fair use of copyright in previous discussions. It is mainly about the necessity of demonstrating "system changes will be brought about by technological changes" from the perspective of economics, i.e., the problem of modification faced by the system of fair use of copyright.

The system of fair use is an outcome under certain technical and economic conditions and should also be appropriately adjusted or restructured as the conditions change. When determining the relevant copyright system on the premise of the legitimacy of the copyright system and that the law should realize sufficient and effective protection of the copyright, we will find that, in the era of digital technology, users can use others' works without paying the price and without restrictions in the name of fair use, and the interests of the rights holders are hollowed out under the umbrella of fair use, in accordance with the principles established by the system of fair use of copyright under the traditional technical conditions. The protection on the interests of the rights holders by laws and even the copyright system itself perform practically no function. Therefore, although it is still too early to talk about whether the system of fair use should be eliminated, the system of fair use must be adjusted significantly in response to changes in order to maintain the survival of the copyright system.

In addition to analyzing the reconfigurations of fair use from the perspective of economics, this book will make an in-depth research on the interactions between legal systems and culture. In the post-industrial era, the cultural form has undergone

Preface

ix

tremendous changes. The development of modern culture characterized by commodification and mediation has largely affected the changes of the legal system. As part of the intellectual property system, the copyright system itself is concerned with a cultural right, which affects people's contact with knowledge and acts on human innovation. The harshness or easing of the system of fair use may have different effects on the direction of cultural development and the innovative manner of people.

This author believes that under the existing copyright system, first of all, it is necessary to stipulate the application of fair use with more stringent standards; secondly, in order to protect the public's interest in the acquisition of knowledge resources, it may be considered to effectively protect the interests of rights holders by expanding the scope of statutory licenses, to reduce the costs of statutory licenses appropriately as a balance and to collectively classify a part of the private copying problems as the copyright limitation category with the statutory licenses; thirdly, it may regulate licensable content for fair use in order to meet the public interest to the public law field; and finally, the fair use may be defined as "innovative capital" existing in the "investment" that encourages innovation, which provides a new perspective for the survival of fair use.

The system of limitation on copyright is a product from an industrialized social environment dominated by early traditional manufacturing. With the development of technology and the transformation of production methods, the relative lag of the system will inevitably become an obstacle to the realization of copyright benefits, and the system is more and more powerless for the moral rights or economic rights in the implementation of the rights. It is a topic worthy of continuous discussion that how the copyright system will reflect the value of its existence in the digital age. How to encourage innovation and achieve balanced distribution of interests in the new system environment is a problem that must be solved by the copyright system.

Law is like the nerve of society. The development of every stage of human society systematically affects the law and adjusts the social relations in revolution by laws. In the post-industrial era, the impact of technology on the economy and the law is more systematic, larger, and even leads to the emergence of a globally unified system. This feature is particularly prominent in the intellectual property legal system. Therefore, the development and reform of the basic system in intellectual property law has transcended the individuality of different countries and regions and has become a common problem facing the world.

As we all know, intellectual property, as a new property form that comes with industrial civilization, is similar to traditional property rights yet has essential differences. The continuous advancement and change of knowledge and technology have profoundly affected our research and mastery on it. Digital technology is a qualitative change and leaps in the progress of human technology. It can be sure that it has profoundly changed our way of life, production methods, behaviors, ways of thinking, and ways of existence, and changed the concepts including traditional time and space, value, and property. We have a reason to believe that it has not yet shown a really significant impact on the social economy, the law, and life. As far as the copyright system is concerned, with the development of copyright content, the system of fair use of copyright must also be adjusted in time and adjusted accordingly. In the process of establishment, operation, and continuous adjustment of the system, fair use is an enduring topic that cannot be put on hold due to unstable boundary. Practice has taught us that the maturity of research on the system of fair use is always relative. Today, the rapid development and wide application of digital technology has broken the structure of the traditional copyright system and poses a very big challenge to this system. It is time for us to put efforts and make a respond.

Since the establishment of the Chinese Copyright Law in 1990, due to the limitations of the legislative system and mechanism, the work of amending the law has lagged behind. In more than 20 years, there were only two amendments to the law in 2001 and 2010, respectively. The activities of amendments to the law cannot keep up with the economic and social development and cannot be compared with developed countries and regions, especially Japan. This is not only a relatively lagging performance of the law but also a reflection of China's backwardness in technological development and economy as a developing country. The essence of legislation and judicature is an important part of social and economic activities. The lag of legislation and the backwardness of the judicial level will affect, hinder, or even constrain economic development and social progress. Whether the intellectual property system is advanced is related to a plurality of fields such as economy, science and technology, and politics of a country. On the occasion of the third revision of this copyright law, by analyzing the impact of digital technology on the production, distribution, circulation, and consumption of knowledge in modern society, this book seeks to further explore the nature and function of fair use, relocate the fair use system, and propose a better plan for the design of China's system of limitation on copyright while readjusting the copyright system.

Beijing, China   Shaojun Liu

Introduction

Since the turn of the millennium, digital technology has been widely applied to every aspect of people's lives. The development of technology is gradually changing trading methods and lifestyles and is impacting and bringing challenges to the traditional intellectual property system. The intellectual property system, as a legal system that encourages innovation and protects inventions and creations, has also undergone many changes with the evolvement and application of technologies. Compared with patents and trademarks, copyright has been changing dramatically on aspects such as the form of works, way of protection, term of protection, and scope and extent of protection. Meanwhile, works, the object protected by the copyright law, also need to be discussed in the digital technology environment, from the creation of works to their use, and from obtaining works to their dissemination. With technical support, the dissemination of works, an embodiment of knowledge, is much easier than ever before. Moreover, the author's control over works also goes from strong to weak, then back to strong again. How to balance the protection of interests of the author and the public is the key to system adjustment and also a core issue of the copyright limitation system.

The system of limitations on copyright initially focused on study of the fair use system. This was followed by discussion on statutory licenses. The final goal is to set up the structure for the system of limitations on copyright. At present, there are abundant theoretical researches and practical experiences at home and abroad concerning the fair use system of copyright. Under the digital technology, fair use has a great impact on rights holders and related industries. The widespread use of digital technology had profound impact on the copyright system and especially had brought about great challenges to the fair use system. This has drawn extensive attention and become an important issue for lawmakers, judges, and researchers. Literatures of current researches mainly cover the following topics: first, theoretical analysis on the fair use nature of copyright; second, rules for the application of the fair use doctrine, with researches on the application of the fair use doctrine in the USA and cases involving this doctrine, and on the evolution of the fair use system and the drafting of law in countries with written copyright laws; third, the status of fair use in the Internet environment; and fourth, composition of the system of limitation on copyright.

Existing research data provides a broad perspective for understanding the experiences and differences in the fair use system of copyright at home and abroad, and the discussion of related topics is an important basis for further researches. However, the main shortcoming of existing research is that they are not systematic. In view of the above, the main research topics of this book are as follows. First, the consensus on the value of the fair use system: this is the premise of understanding the value and legitimacy of the system and is the basis for systematic discussion and research. Second, fair use offers coordination and interaction with the property rights in the copyright system to balance the interests between rights holders and users.

Traditionally, it is considered that reasonable limitations on the copyright are the same as the exclusion of copyright, and fair use itself can also stimulate innovation, which makes it necessary to systematically study the copyright system. Third, and the primary focus of this book is, in the digital technology environment, how can we set reasonable limitations on copyright in order to protect the interests of the rights holders and at the same time ensure the freedom of "use" by the public in this new media age, and how to eventually balance interests of all parties.

Domestic and foreign rights holders have implemented new business models to adapt to the new digital technology environment. These business models have made it challenging to maintain the fair use system. This book compares different legislative models, draws on the management and operation experience of other countries, and summarizes theoretical deficiencies and practical dilemmas of the current system of China. Suggestions on improvement are provided, with an aim to shed some light on solving both historical and current problems, and on the design the future look of the system of copyright limitation in China.

This book mainly consists of the following three parts.

The first part introduces the theoretical basis of the fair use system. The nature and legitimacy of the system are analyzed from the theoretical perspective. Existing literature has done in-depth analysis on this issue from different levels. This book intends to analyze the logical starting points of various viewpoints and conclusions, distinguish the theories in different fields, and analyze the legal relationship in the fair use system based on an analysis of the legal relationship in the copyright system.

The second part analyzes the status and role of the fair use system in the copyright system in different periods by exploring the evolution of the fair use system in several countries. The study on the fair use system should be based on the practices in China. However, foreign experience, systems, and theories may also be used as reference. This book introduces copyright-related legislations in the USA, Britain, Canada, Germany, Japan, and other countries, and the amendments made by these countries to adapt to technological changes. Using the experience of many countries as a basis, the history, current situation, and future of the fair use system are analyzed. Further, the legal relationship of fair use in the copyright system is systematically analyzed. By such analysis, we study the subtle changes of the status of fair use caused by the change in the rights and obligations relations due to technological revolution in the copyright system, whether under a traditional institutional framework, or in digital technology environment, and seek to find a reasonable position for the fair use system under the new communication technology.

The third part involves reflection on and reconstruction of the fair use system in China. For the institutional research, we should be able to adapt to changes, introduce new ideas, and analyze and find the theory to solve the problems faced by fair use in technological reforms from the perspective of economics and public interest. In studying the issue of statutory license, we discuss the copyright collective management system and the role that the system should play and the corresponding design that should be made in the legislation.

Research Methodologies

First, empirical analysis. This book is a research on system rather than a theoretical research. Therefore, the study should be based on institutional norms and practical operational problems and try to find deviations from the original intentions and institutional dilemmas, so as to carry out targeted research. Therefore, as writing this book, I collected the material on practical cases, especially cases from USA and UK, and analyzed the rules for the application of the fair use doctrine with some US and UK cases.

Second, analysis of law and economic. This method is commonly used for providing efficiency analysis in institutional analysis and is convinced in efficiency and rationality. The economic analysis method in transaction cost theory has been the most widely accepted theory that can make a reasonable way out for fair use behavior. When fair use occurs, in the context of the traditional modes of communication, market failures caused by excessively high transaction cost may prevent the rights holders from obtaining profits or cause the users to abandon their use due to excessively high licensing costs. In the new technology environment, however, technological advancement can solve the problem of excessively high transaction costs. Further, the application of digital technology can facilitate rights holder's authorization and the user's payment of consideration. The reduction in transaction costs maybe a fatal blow to the existence of the fair use system. Therefore, the method of economic analysis will reposition the fair use system in the copyright system.

Third, comparative analysis. Comparative analysis is an important method of self-cognition. Only after various comparisons, can we fully understand the progress and deficiencies we have. Chinese copyright system is borrowed from abroad. The fair use system is a system with great controversy, with the regulations of different countries vastly different. In China's copyright system, the composition of the limitation system on copyright had been improved. By comparative analysis, we can better define the deficiencies in law. For this purpose, the comparative analysis method will be more targeted and credible, and conclusions from such analysis will be more convincing. Of course, with regard to the comparative analysis method, we should be cautious in sample selection. We need to evaluate whether to select all samples or to extract some samples, and to select samples on criteria. The samples used in this book are the systems of UK, USA, Germany, France, and Italy. On the base of differences in

xiv   Introduction

the definition of works, it is more representative to analyze the systems in different regions with the same legal origin.

Structure and Content

The Preface mainly covers basic issues such as research basis, background, content, research methodologies, and innovation points.

Chapter 1 discusses the theoretical basis of the limitations on copyright.

In introducing the overall framework of the fair use system, this chapter discusses the nature and legitimacy of fair use, and focuses on the relationship between fair use, a doctrine in the copyright law, and copyright and other rights.

Several theories on the nature of fair use are introduced, including the theories of rights limitation, justifiable cause, user rights, and legal interest that is not yet right. The ideas of these theories are reviewed. The legitimacy of the fair use system is discussed from the perspectives of the philosophy of intellectual property law, economics, constitutional law, and sociology. As copyright is a property right, and the existence of the fair use system is supported by the transaction cost theory, this chapter focuses on the impact of the economic analysis method on the fair use system and the changes brought about by new technologies. From the perspective of sociology, this chapter further discusses the characteristics of cultural modernization and its relationship and interaction with the legal system.

Chapter 2 discusses the institutional context of the fair use system and analyzes the application of fair use through a comparison of laws in different countries. The first part of this chapter introduces the legislation and judicial practice of the fair use system in case law countries that adopt "essentialism" as the core and analyzes the establishment for the fair use doctrine, with a focus on US cases. The second part introduces the legislation of the countries and regions in the continental law system. The third part introduces the fair use system based on the three-step test in international treaties. The fourth part introduces the legislation in China on the basis of two fair use cases.

Chapter 3 begins with an analysis of the legal relationship of the copyright system and further analyzes the subject of rights, object of rights, and the legal relationship between the subject and object in the fair use system.

Chapter 4 attempts to classify the limitations on copyright in the digital technology environment. First, the definition and types of private copying are introduced. Second, the status and role of the copying for innovation in the fair use system are analyzed. In addition, the status of different forms of works in the fair use system is discussed.

Chapter 5 discusses the reconstruction of the copyright limitation system. Legislations in other countries reflect the particularity of the digital technology environment. Reframing the rights limitation system is further provided in this chapter. First, this chapter demonstrates why digital technology has begun to shake the foundation of the fair use system. In view that the legitimacy of the system proved by the transaction cost theory is questioned, the role of disseminators is becoming increasingly important in the market relationship. This not only determines the distribution of interests but also plays an increasingly important role in issues such as culture, value, and aesthetic trends. Thus, we should pay more attention to the status and role of disseminators in the framework of the copyright limitation system. The solution may be to further expand the range of statutory license so that the rights holder can be better rewarded.

Chapter 6 is a discussion of the copyright collective management system. It provides an in-depth analysis on the protection of rights holders' benefits through statutory licenses and analyzes problems such as licensing standards.

Chapter 7 is entitled "Code is Law." Based on an analysis of the latest technology, this chapter aims to judge the trend of the legal system and to shed some light on how to design a forward-looking system in China that can adapt to the development of digital economy.

Contents

1 Theoretical Basis for the Rights Limitation System 1
    1.1 Theoretical Basis for Fair Use 1
        1.1.1 Definition of Fair Use 1
        1.1.2 Nature of Fair Use 2
    1.2 Arguments on the Legitimacy of the Fair Use System 6
        1.2.1 Essence of Intellectual Property 7
        1.2.2 Economic Analysis 13
        1.2.3 Constitutional Analysis 18
        1.2.4 Sociological Analysis 22
    References 28

2 Legislative Status of the Fair Use System 31
    2.1 Case Law Countries 32
        2.1.1 United States 32
        2.1.2 United Kingdom 36
        2.1.3 Canada 39
    2.2 Civil Law Countries 41
        2.2.1 Germany 41
        2.2.2 Japan 42
    2.3 International Treaties 43
    2.4 Legislation in China 45
        2.4.1 Laws 45
        2.4.2 Cases Involving Fair Use 47
    References 51

3 Legal Relationship of the Rights Limitation System 53
    3.1 Legal Relationship of the Copyright System 53
        3.1.1 Subject 54
        3.1.2 Object 55
        3.1.3 Applications 56
        3.1.4 Relationship Between Rights and Obligations 60
    3.2 Legal Relationship of the Fair Use System 60
        3.2.1 Subject 60

xvii

	3.2.2	Object	60
	3.2.3	Application	61
	3.2.4	Relationship Between Rights and Obligations	62
	References		62

4 Types of Rights Limitation in Digital Technology Environment 65

4.1 Private Copying 66

    4.1.1 Classification of Private Copying 66

    4.1.2 Definition of Private Copying 67

    4.1.3 The Significance of Imposing Strict Limitations
on of Private Copying Behavior in Fair Use 68

    4.1.4 Compensation System 69

    4.1.5 Private Copying for Musical Works 70

4.2 Copying for Innovation Purpose 73

    4.2.1 Copying for Innovation Purpose 73

    4.2.2 Relationship Between Rational Use and Innovation 74

    4.2.3 Fair Use and Parody 78

References 82

5 Reconstruction of the Rights Limitation System 83

5.1 Impact of Digital Technology on Current Legal System 83

    5.1.1 Digital Technology Eliminates Market Failures
Caused by Excessively High Transaction Costs 83

    5.1.2 Trends in Social and Cultural Development Require
the Continuation of the Fair Use System 84

5.2 Establishment of Digital Rights Management Systems 86

    5.2.1 Digital Rights Management 86

    5.2.2 Temporary Reproduction 88

    5.2.3 Legal Liabilities of Network Operators 90

5.3 Statutory License 94

    5.3.1 Definition and Function of Statutory License 94

    5.3.2 Legislation in Some Countries 95

5.4 Restructuring of the System of Copyright Limitations 97

    5.4.1 Strictly Limit the Scope of Fair Use 98

    5.4.2 Expanding the Scope of Statutory License 99

    5.4.3 Business Transformation Achieved by Strict Rights
Limitations and Strong Rights Protections 100

    5.4.4 Establishing a "Fair Use" Welfare System Rooted
in the Public Law System 102

References 104

**6 Improvement of Copyright Collective Management System
in Statutory License** 107

6.1 Concept of Copyright Collective Management System 107

6.2 Status Quo of China's Copyright Collective Management
System 110

	6.2.1	Extended Collective Management System 111
	6.2.2	Royalty Rates 114
Reference 115		

7 Code Is Law 117
7.1 Digital Technology Reshaping Economic Behavior 117
7.2 Distributed Storage Protecting Rights 119
7.3 Smart Contracts Guaranteeing Fair Trade 120
7.4 Conclusions 121
References 122

About the Translators

Shibao Wang after graduation with a master degree of Biochemistry and Molecular Biology from Zhejiang Sci-Tech University and Joint-Supervision from Biotechnology Research Institute, CAAS, has been a professional translator at IPPH for 9 years. She has accumulated rich experience in translating documents on IP legislation. She translated a book (published, co-translator), *Technology Transfer and Intellectual Property Issues*.

An Zhang graduated from Shandong University of TCM with a BA Degree in English has been working as a translator at IPPH, engaged to patent translation in the field of mechanics, communication, etc. for almost 9 years. He has built his own understanding about translation, IP, and relevant laws during his career. He has also devoted some efforts for translation teaching to share his experience and IP knowledge in some universities.

Hao Wang after graduation from Renmin University of China, with a bachelor degree of Physics and a master degree of English Language Literature, began her career as a patent attorney in 2010. She had been working as a patent attorney in law firms for 8 years and obtained her patent practicing certificate in 2015. From 2018, she has worked as a skilled translator regarding intellectual property and has acquired considerable experience in translation related to IP legislation.

Jie Wang upon graduation from Northeast Normal University with a master degree began her career as a translator. She has gathered extensive experience and gained a good command of skills in years of translation pertaining to intellectual property, especially to patent documents. Now, she serves as a project manager, responsible for scheduling translation projects comprehensively. Besides, she translated this book in her pregnancy and felt quite amazing to accomplish such a job while waiting for a new life, as this translation of the book was just like another baby of hers.

Chapter 1
Theoretical Basis for the Rights Limitation System

This chapter introduces the compositions of the fair use system and clarifies the definition and characteristics of the system. Fair use is an "exemption" in the entire copyright system, or an "exception" to the absolute right of the copyright holder. Research on the system of rights limitation initially starts from the study of fair use. Therefore, to clarify the fundamental theories of the fair use system is the basis to build a framework of the rights limitation system. This chapter also illustrates the reasons why the fair use system came into being and the legitimacy of the system in the traditional copyright system, and provides a theoretical basis for further study of the status and changes of the system of rights limitation in the digital age.

1.1 Theoretical Basis for Fair Use

1.1.1 Definition of Fair Use

Fair use is the right to use copyrighted works in accordance with the relevant provisions of the law without the consent of the copyright owner, or payment of remuneration to the copyright owner. However, the copyright owner's moral right to works should be respected.[1] As a limitation on copyright, fair use mainly reflects the limitations on rights holders from the perspective of economic interests. At the same time, the law also imposes very strict rules on fair use behaviors. Common law countries establish the fair use system by setting up rules for the application of fair use, while continental law countries establish the fair use system by enumerating the specific behaviors of copyright owners that are prohibited by the copyright law.

---

[1] Li and Xu [1].

© Intellectual Property Publishing House 2021
S. Liu, *Rights Limitation in Digital Age*,
https://doi.org/10.1007/978-981-16-4380-4_1

1.1.2 Nature of Fair Use

Scholars at home and abroad define the nature of fair use from the perspective of either rights holders or users. The main theories in this regard include the theories of rights limitation, justifiable cause, user rights and legal interests.

1.1.2.1 Rights Limitation

The rights limitation theory states that fair use is a limitation on the property rights of works as stipulated by law.

The general idea of rights limitation is mainly rooted in Kant's point of view. Kant believes that the limitation on public power is aimed at ensuring that the exercise of rights does not harm the legitimate interests of others. However, as copyright is a property right that is different from real right, to set limitations on copyright is to set rights holders "obligations" under specific circumstances inside the rights system. In addition to national interests, public interests, and public order and customs that restrict the exercising of rights, the law also provides additional, explicit, and specific limitations on the scope of rights that copyright owners can exercise.[2] The theory of rights limitation states that the author's rights on his work are not completely exclusive. This premise of this theory negates the integrity and absolute status of rights under copyright. "The theory of rights limitations is not possible for the user of the work to provide a cause for requesting for a certain action from the rights holder of the work".[3] This theory is essentially from the perspective of the rights holder.

"The rights limitation theory, as a generally accepted theory on fair use in the intellectual property theory, is rational to some extent. The reason that fair use is regarded as a limitation on the property rights of works is that copyright is exclusive in essence. To allow use of other people's works without permission is a limitation or restriction on copyright. Some scholars believe that when a user's behavior is fair use, his behavior does not constitute a violation to the rights of the copyright owner. The user has no right to, and cannot make any claims against the copyright owner. Only when the copyright owner accuses the user of infringement can the user use fair use defense."[4] Under the digital technology, copyright owners can use technical measures to prevent users' "fair" use behavior that is unauthorized and unpaid for; users may not use the "rights limitation theory" to require the copyright owner to waive a part of their monopoly right, and may not receive any relief on the ground of "rights limitation" with regard to the various measures adopted by copyright owners.

---

[2] Liu [2].

[3] Sun [3].

[4] Dong [4].

1.1 Theoretical Basis for Fair Use

1.1.2.2 Justifiable Cause

This theory claims that fair use is a justifiable cause for a copyright violation.[5] The premise of this theory is that the boundary of copyright is complete, and the rights of copyright owners are composed of two types of rights: prohibition right and the right to remuneration. Namely, any use should be approved by the rights holders or should pay remuneration to rights holders, otherwise it constitutes infringement. However, due to the special provisions of the law, these behaviors are not defined as infringement, but exceptions. This theory first assumes that fair use is an infringement. However, because there are special provisions in law, the illegality is invalid. It is believed by this theory that fair use is a statutory defense against copyright infringement accusations. "Japanese scholar Katsumoto Masaakira believes that the fair use of rights is essentially an unlawful behavior, but as its illegality is invalidated, such behavior should not be viewed as illegal. At the same time, the causes to justify such behavior should be directly stipulated by law. In addition, he believes that based on the principle of the Japanese Constitution that gives priority to the public interests, the purpose for the limitations on copyright is to prevent the abuse of copyright, and to allow others to properly use works, i.e., the fair use of rights."[6] This theory in effect uses constituent elements of an infringement to analyze the status and effect of fair use, and thus to determine whether a use constitute infringement. Superficially, fair use seems to have the effect of justify illegal behavior, but we cannot bluntly view fair use as the cause that justifies illegal behavior. That is to say, although a behavior that conforms to the constituent elements is illegal in nature, however, it is not considered illegal if such a behavior is an exception provided by law. This theory first views a fair use behavior as an infringement, and then presumes that such an illegality is invalid only because the law stipulates so. China scholar Zhang Jing believes that "a fair use behavior is in essence an infringement, but it is not determined as infringement after the source is indicated", "the only difference between fair use and compulsory license is that the former does not need to pay remuneration while the latter requires payment. Since compulsory authorization is a justifiable cause, fair use shall also be such a cause".[7] "The justifiable cause is an important concept in the continental law system. It refers to the cause that obstructs the illegality of a behavior that conforms to the constituting elements of a crime."[8] "Exemption of tort" in the tort law system is different from the concept of "defense". The exemption of tort liabilities, also known as the conditions for the exemption of tort liabilities, refers to a situation in which the tort liability can be exempted or mitigated.[9] Defense, however, is a concept in the common law system, and it refer to a fact based on which defendant asserts that the plaintiff's claim cannot be established or fully established, and that his civil liability should be exempted or mitigated. To go one step further,

---

[5] Wu [5].

[6] Quoted from Wu [5, 6].

[7] Quoted from Wu [7].

[8] Zhang [8].

[9] Chang and Feng [9].

the consequences of such use behavior does not harm the interests of rights holders. Thus, to judge whether this theory is rational, the premise is to estimate whether the fair use behavior is illegal and whether it has adverse consequences of harming the interests of rights holders. The illegality of a behavior must satisfy two conditions: First, the law provides that regarding certain rights and interests of the rights holder, other party have the obligation not to infringe; and second, the behavior of such other party violates the obligation and causes damage to the rights holder. The scope and extent of fair use behavior are clearly stipulated in the law, that is, the behavior is not considered illegal by law. But objectively, fair use in essence "infringes" the interests of the rights holder. This theory is mainly from the user's point of view, and is based on defenses in litigation practice. It is a supplementary explanation of the "rights limitation theory" from the perspective of the users.

1.1.2.3 User Rights Theory

Professor Wu Handong believes that fair use is not an infringement and is not illegal in form, thus denying the "justifiable cause" theory. Both the "rights limitations" and "exemption of tort" theories argue that fair use is an exception to copyright and is defense against infringement accusation. The "user rights" theory considers that fair use is an independent right of the user of works, and the copyright owner has to bear corresponding obligations. However, if fair use is determined as a "user right", there is an insurmountable contradiction: according to the principle of civil law, civil rights and obligations are the core of civil legal relations, and any civil legal relations are relations of civil rights and obligations. In this relation, rights and obligations are relative. Thus, in the fair use relations, the subject of a right enjoys the rights, and the subject of an obligation undertakes the obligations. If the user is a rights holder, the subject of a right may be many unspecified people, while the copyright owner as an obligor is a specific obligation subject, who has an obligation of not acting against a fair user's exercises of copyright. This is contrary to the exclusiveness of copyright, and is also contradictory to basic rules of the civil law that says "the subject of a right in the same civil legal relationship shall be specified, while the subject of obligation can be unspecified".

The user rights theory claims that fair use is a privilege for users to use works in a fair manner without the consent of the author, and is an independent right of users to use the protected works of others according to law. From the perspective of the subject in the fair use relationship, this theory believes that the rights obtained from fair use is a user's privilege, and emphasizes that fair use is a right granted to the user by law. "The behavior of using the work of others is set as the right of the user", that is, in the circumstance of meeting the conditions (for determining fair use), the user has the right to use the work.[10] Logically, this seems to violate the integrity of the "copyright" and neglect the attributes of copyright. That is, if the right is established, it should not be based on the work and should not be attributed

---

[10] Wu [7].

1.1 Theoretical Basis for Fair Use

to be within the framework of the copyright right, because its rights generation is not derived from the extension of the concept of private rights. The subject of right does not match with the subject of obligation.[11] American scholars L. Ray Patterson and Stanley W. Lindberg stated in the book *The Nature of Copyright: A Law of User' Rights* that "modern copyright law is a product from balancing the rights between creators, publishers and users"; "it is reasonably believed that the copyright law, as a legal system, must pay attention to the rights of all individuals in the process of creating, disseminating and using works;" "the users also have the right. Denying the use right of individuals will lead to control over the public by the copyright, with a result of seeking so-called economic benefits for a few people." "If the copyright law is to serve the public interests, it must be inclusive of two private rights that often conflict—a right of the economic return of his work for that the creator disseminates to the public and a right of a user to learn by using the work to improve his or her knowledge."[12]

1.1.2.4 Legal Interests

The legal interests refer to the interests that have not been or cannot be categorized but should be protected by law in real life. Different from the type of rights that have been defined in law, namely "typed freedom", legal interests is low in legal effect compared to legal rights. When law cannot exhaust all rights by its rules, it can protect certain interests by setting up certain principles. Liszt pointed out: "Legal interests are the interests protected by law. All legal interests are life-related interests, and they are the interests of individuals or the society. It is not the law order but the life that produces this kind of interests, and the protection of law is to increase the life interests to the legal interests."[13]

Some believe that fair use should be legal interests that cannot be categorized; the subject that enjoys this legal interest is not the rights holder but the user; and this legal interest should be restricted to the user's own use and prohibit circulation.[14] Some holds that the theory of legal interests does not involve the discussion on the legal relationship, breaks away from the limitation of "rights", and is an argument from the perspective of jurisprudence. The discussion of interests always involves trade-offs and compromises, while, rights are a matter of principle that requires an uncompromising attitude.[15] This author believes that classifying fair use as legal interest which is relatively vague in concept further enlarges the uncertainty of the fair use system. Whether it is positioned as "rights" or interpreted as "legal interests", it is necessary to clarify the relationship between the various elements in the system. Only by systematically analyzing the legal relationship in the system can legislator

---

[11] See Footnote 4.

[12] Patterson and Lindberg [10], quoted from Jonathan [11].

[13] Zhang [12].

[14] See Footnote 3.

[15] Holmes and Sunstein [13], p. 68.

balance the interests of each subject and can the judge weigh the interests of each party and the impact of the judgment on the society on a case by case basis.

1.1.2.5 Summary

This author believes that as fair use is an important doctrine in the system of limitation on copyright, the definition to its nature should be based on the copyright owner's point of view. Due to the provisions of law, the copyright owner has to take apart from his rights and let the user enjoy it free of charge. This is a form of rights limitation and a way to restrict monopoly rights. The justifiable cause is another explanation of rights limitation, and the two expressions complement each other. The theory of user rights tends to explain the nature of fair use from the perspective of the public. However, as the copyright owners are the subject of the copyright law, it seems wired to view the public as the subject of interests in the fair use system, which is a private law concept. In this aspect, it is more appropriate to explain fair use based on the freedom of speech in the constitution. The theory of legal interests is an objective interpretation of the existence of fair use behavior, and cannot answer the question of the nature of fair use. Therefore, I support the using of the rights limitation theory to explain the nature of fair use.

1.2 Arguments on the Legitimacy of the Fair Use System

In order to ensure that rights holders use their intellectual property exclusively and make others use the works under certain conditions, it is necessary to give the rights owners the monopoly right and at the same time impose necessary limitations on their rights. For these purposes, different authorization methods should be designed to improve the entire system, including authorized use, statutory license or compulsory license and fair use. The behavior of copying a protected work without the permission of the rights holder is in effect an infringement on the ownership of the copyright owner, and "the law needs to prove that such 'trauma' and limitations on rights are justified; and at the same time, the most important one in these reasons is the concept of competitive rights."[16] In the fair use system, public interest is a factor that competes with copyright owner's private rights. A copyright limitation system is needed to control its over-monopoly status. Meanwhile, fair use should be based on the legitimate interests of the copyright owner. Of course, by setting boundary of fair use, the rights of rights holders will be directly affected. "If the rights are not subject to any limitations, it will be harmful".[17] Therefore, the application of fair use should be subject to more stringent conditions.

---

[16] Korematsu v. United States, 323 US 214 (1944). See Holmes and Sunstein [13], p. 69.

[17] Holmes and Sunstein [13], p. 69.

1.2.1 Essence of Intellectual Property

To study the essence of fair use, it is necessary to analyze the essence of intellectual property. This is because fair use is within the scope of the copyright system. The limitation on copyright and the legitimacy of copyrights form a contradictory relationship. It is thus necessary to discuss the legitimacy of intellectual property. After the legitimacy is proved, we can then analyze and explain why the law imposes certain limitations on copyright, a property right that has the attributes of private rights.

1.2.1.1 Natural Rights

(1)   Separation of intellectual property right and real right

"If people want to assert intellectual property right, they must first create something with a certain meaning, in other words, something that can be expressed. Then they should attach it to some material carrier so that it can be specific."[18]

Artistic creation is a kind of accession behavior implemented on objects. As one of the most basic expressions of ownership, the traditional definition of accession refers to a combination of objects owned by different people to form an inseparable object or a new object. If it is virtually impossible or economically unreasonable to restore the object, the ownership of this new object needs to be determined. The behavior of accomplishing the expression of res incorporales on res corporales is a kind of accession behavior. By combining two kinds of property on the same object, the author changes the objective form and value of the res corporales which then conveys new contents. The recognition of intellectual property can be traced back to a record on the author's status in ancient Rome. According to the record, a painter drew on a table which belonged to others, and then the painter and the owner of the table had a dispute over the ownership of the table. The judge held that the value of the painting was higher than that of the table, so the painter owned this table.[19] This is a typical example that accession behavior adds value to the original object and changes the ownership of the object.

However, intellectual property is not born with the real right system, and no system recognizes this kind of incorporeal property brought about by knowledge. This is mainly because, in the era of handicraft, both the form of "beauty" attached to an object and the knowledge that can be transmitted by the object are transferred with the transfer of real rights, whether it is the creation of artists or the labour of craftsmen. The interests from the acquisition of knowledge are included in the interests derived from the acquisition of real rights. It is difficult to separate the two. For example, paintings and sculptures are traded because of their beautiful form, but such form is difficult to be copied (or can only be copied at a high cost). Another

---

[18] Yu [14], p. 381.

[19] "The ABC of Copyright" UNESCO.

example is the copying of books. In the era of hand-written books, only those books on religion, philosophy, etc. were in written forms. Books were circulated within a very small range and at a very low frequency. Furthermore, few people can afford books or read books. When a work is sold, all rights on this work are lost with the transfer of the real right. The significance of the technological revolution lies in that it frees the hands of human beings and enables industrialized production to reproduce a creation of human beings by technical means. Therefore, the creating of a work for the first time is called creation, while reproduction is called manufacture and production. Industrial revolution enables creators to create a work and reproduce it. When a work becomes a product, creation is distinguished and placed at a prominent position, and becomes an independent element that can generate wealth.

In the realm of real rights, transaction means the exchange of property and also the exchange of property rights. Because both property and the related rights are directed at an object existent itself. The uniqueness of an object determines that the transaction of an object is the transaction of related rights; however, the transaction of intellectual property is separated from the object, and its right is realized by being continuously copied on new carriers without affecting the value of the object. This is inversely proportional to the economic scarcity of natural objects. When knowledge, as a product, is separated from the object, it has the following characteristics: "(1) It is difficult for producers of knowledge to control the products from knowledge innovation. If the creator hides his knowledge products, his innovation activities will not be recognized, and will have no social significance. If it is made public, it is difficult to effectively control this intangible resource. (2) Consumption of knowledge products by one person will not affect the consumption of others, and one public information resource can be shared by as many people as possible. (3) Knowledge products are a transient asset. The production of information comes at a price, while the cost to transmit information is very low. Once the producer sells his or her information to the consumer, the consumer becomes the producer's potential competitor, and other consumers may become free riders that take advantage of the information. (4) The consumption of knowledge products is different from that of other public products. The use of knowledge products will not produce tangible wastage so as to reduce the knowledge products. On the contrary, it may expand the total amount of intangible resources of society. However, due to "externality", the information provided by producers is often freely used by consumers. Although this may result in a much higher social benefits from knowledge products compared with the benefits obtained by creators, it is difficult for the producers of knowledge products to recover costs by selling information."[20]

Therefore, the intellectual wealth that human "creates" can accumulate by technology and can increase economic benefits. This makes people to face the source of creating such wealth, pay attention to the power of first innovation, and recognize the dominant position of the author regarding his property rights. Therefore, an intellectual property system emerges to protect such property right. Within the traditional intellectual property framework, copyright owners are concerned with the creation of

---

[20] Cao et al. [15].

1.2 Arguments on the Legitimacy of the Fair Use System

new knowledge. Their control over their rights and calculation of economic benefits are achieved by controlling copying behaviors and counting the number of copies.

(2) Essence of property rights

In Second Treatises of Government, Locke answers the question "why can a man gain property rights?" Locke's theory has a theological basis that "God has arranged everything". He then explains the reason why God so distributes "property" based on the labour theory. First, human has the ownership of himself or herself; and second, by dictating his or her body to work, he or she obtains property. "So when he takes something from the state that nature has provided and left it in, he mixes his labour with it, thus joining to it something that is his own; and in that way he makes it his property. He has removed the item from the common state that nature has placed it in, and through this labour the item has had annexed to it something that excludes the common right of other men: for this labour is unquestionably the property of the labourer, so no other man can have a right to anything the labour is joined to—at least where there is enough, and as good, left in common for others."[21] The role of labour in the formation of private property can only be satisfied during the natural state when Adam and Eve were just driven out of the Garden of Eden. God's request to mankind was only to let people earn their own living. As there were abundant resources, mankind did not need to worry about economic issues.

The premise of Locke's property rights is that everything in the world comes from God, and they are owned by mankind in common; that property right indirectly refers to the exclusive possession of a part that people take from the commonly owned object.[22] Further, Locke believes that the government has the power to regulate property, but this power must be consistent with the goals of the law of nature. In making normative decisions, the government should provide alternative options.[23] This means that the natural rights of property are not "sacred and inviolable", but an adjustable interest relationship and an instrument-based right. Therefore, the theory of natural rights based on Locke's theory is questionable.

Creative activity itself does not generate property rights. By creative activity, an author transforms the right to use public knowledge into an exclusive right based on a creative product (a work). In the view of labour-based natural property rights, the doctrine of "sweat of the brow" becomes a sole criterion in judging when we can view the part of knowledge that is separated from public resources as the object of intellectual property.

Labor does not play a leading role in the history of human wealth accumulation. Pufendorf believes that when people take property from res communes given by God, the way they rely on is mutual agreement, and it is constantly adjusted according to the condition, nature of the object, and the number of human beings.[24] British judge Aston believes that the existence of copyright is mainly based on "the fact that an

---

[21] Locke [16].

[22] Drahos [17], pp. 56–57.

[23] Tully [18], quoted from Drahos [17], pp. 56–57.

[24] Tully [18], quoted from Drahos [17], p. 59.

author has rights to the products of his mental creations". He believes that "This kind of property is essentially different from the property acquired by possession. The property obtained by possession is originally owned by all, not by you. You obtained the property by your personal behavior. This property originally belongs to the author. Therefore, the property should still belong to him. Unless by his own actions and with his own full agreement, the property is expressly given it to everyone."[25] To solve the problem of possession, in addition to considering the labour factor, both trading habits and agreements of the interest groups are indispensable factors in determining the boundaries of rights.

1.2.1.2 Instrument Theory

The instrumentalist attitude includes the following three aspects: first, it pays attention to the effect of property as an institutional mechanism on social life, rather than its metaphysical, ethical or epistemological aspects; second, it focuses on the realm analytical method of law; in doing cost-benefit analysis, it welcomes morals and emotions rather than reject them; third, it serves certain moral media and is humanism oriented. Instrumentalism treats intellectual property as a privilege, not just a right. Therefore, various restrictive obligations are imposed on this privilege so as to realize the original intention of this privilege as much as possible, and to reach a balance of protection of personal interests and public interests.[26]

"In the past few centuries, the concept of property has changed dramatically in both common law and continental law countries. In traditional law, neither the property rights in the common law nor those in the continental law involve people's intellectual achievements (at least in the institutional level)."[27] In 1557, Queen Mary of Britain granted the printing license to the London Book Publishing Association, which both facilitated the royal family's demand for information control, and satisfied the desire for the monopoly of the printing industry that fears competition. "Britain controls the book trade by granting the privilege to other parties due to the reciprocity between the two interests."[28] The reason for the destruction of this franchise system is partly because the conflict of interests within the industry, which has caused trade imbalances, hence the later Queen Anne Law (hereinafter referred to as the Statute of Anne). Although the Statute of Anne in 1710 is considered an epoch-making law and the first copyright law in the world, the social environment at that time does not give the author the status of an economic subject who can achieve social benefits by performing independent, special, and creative activities. When an author sells his manuscript to others, he no longer has any rights to the original manuscript.[29] This law was originally titled "An Act for the Encouragement of Learning, by vesting the

---

[25] British Judges' Judgment Collection, Volume 9.

[26] Yu [14], p. 387.

[27] Li [19], p. 189.

[28] Drahos [17], p. 33.

[29] Rose [20].

1.2 Arguments on the Legitimacy of the Fair Use System

Copies of Printed Books in the Authors or purchasers of such Copies, during the Times before mentioned." It does not appear to be a law centered on the interests of booksellers. According to Patterson and Lindbergh, the Statute of Anne changed the instrument of monopoly used by publishers and the tool of censorship used by the country into a rule of trade. This change aims to promote knowledge learning and control the monopoly of publishers.[30] The Statute of Anne also stipulates that "under the old system, all literary works will always belong to certain booksellers, and only literary works that have been examined by the booksellers to meet the censorship standards can be published." In concept, the manuscript of a work is the work itself, and the transfer of the manuscript is only a transfer of real rights.

Judge Yates, who believes in the concept of instrumentalism, puts forward a view opposite to that of Judge Aston. He believes that property is built on possession, and abstract objects cannot be possessed. Therefore, it is against the general principle of property to set an abstract real right on thoughts. However, to be fair, an author should be given a certain reward. The limited monopoly rights provided by the Statute of Anne achieve the purpose of reward, conform to the requirements of fairness, and can encourage academic and research activities.[31] The United States Code defines copyright as "providing authors with an instrument that can be used to protect their work from unauthorized possession, use, or use without their permission."[32] Judge Hughes also emphasized that, in American law, the primary object in conferring the monopoly lie in the general benefits derived by the public from the labors of authors.[33] These views highlight the purpose of the copyright system and emphasize the real benefits that such a monopoly system brings to rights holders. Therefore, the copyright system is an instrument to effectively balance the interests of all groups. The copyright system promises to give artists and authors a reasonable return on labor, thereby stimulating their desires for expression and creation. Nowadays, in the digital technology environment, for enterprises or network companies that rely on digital technology to survive, they need the protection of an intellectual property system to help them survive and develop. Therefore, viewing the intellectual property system as an instrument will likely improve the criteria of lawmakers in designing the system with regard to technological change, and make full use of the characteristics of instrumentalism to balance the interests of all parties involved in the change.

1.2.1.3 Natural Rights or Instrument

Traditionally, the legislative purpose of the US intellectual property system is based on instrumentalism, with the most prominent manifestation that the US law does not clearly define the protection of the author's moral rights. This author believes that

---

[30] See Footnote 12.

[31] Drahos [17], pp. 37–38.

[32] The United States Code, Title 17, Section 106 (17 U. S. C. § 106.).

[33] Fox Film Corp v. Doyal, 286 U. S. (1932).

the copyright protection system of the US should be examined with a broader view, rather than from the sole perspective of the copyright law.

From the perspective of the value choice by American cultural, the US Copyright Act is more focused on the "individuals", and aims to establish a system that encourages individual contributions. Similar as the purpose statements in international treaties and the copyright laws of many other countries, China's Copyright Law also says that "the system is established in order to encourage innovation and promote social development and flourishing" in the general provisions of the law. However, these purposes are only used to show that the establishment of the copyright system is justified, rather than to explain the reasons to establish the copyright system.

Grotius, the founder of classical natural law theory, believes that law is a rule discovered by human beings after rational thinking. "In order to become knowledge, the law should not be based on experiences, but on definition; and it should not be based on facts, but on logical deduction. In terms of this standard, only natural law can constitute knowledge. This knowledge must be constructed by completely setting aside everything that changes with time and place."[34]

The process of drawing the rules of law is a process of concepts formation. As Einstein emphasizes, concepts is the products of free thinking through perception.[35] He said: "As long as these principles which are to serve as a starting point for deduction, individual empirical facts are useless to theorists;"[36] and law, as a complete system obtained through rational thinking, "can achieve the truth of theoretical thinking only by considering the relationship between theoretical thinking with a total sum of sensory experience materials."[37]

The core value of the intellectual property system is protection and creation. It is based on human's "natural rights". The purpose for the establishment of the system is that innovation is natural right, and when innovation brings benefits, the benefit should be attributed to the person who implements this innovation. The United States Declaration of Independence states that "it is one of several unalienable rights endowed by the Creator, and the intellectual property system is established to protect this right". Innovation brings about social development, and institutional guarantees encourage innovation. There is a view that the legitimacy of the fair use system is based on the existence of copyright, and the behavior of fair use should be based on a legally acquired copy of the work. Thus the legitimacy of the fair use can be proved by demonstrating the legitimacy of copyright system.[38]

Patterson and Lindberg believe that, the Statute of Anne is originally enacted with the intent of formulating a trade rule that is irrelevant to the philosophical and theoretical foundations we are discussing now, "by asserting that copyright is fundamentally a regulatory concept, a statutory grant of a limited monopoly—not

---

[34] d'Entrbves [21].

[35] Zhou [22].

[36] The Albert Einstein Collection [23], p. 75.

[37] The Albert Einstein Collection [23], p. 523.

[38] Xu [24].

1.2 Arguments on the Legitimacy of the Fair Use System

the author's natural law property right by reason of creation. But this result is from confusing understanding of the nature of copyright: one theory that the copyright originates from the creation of works; and in another view, it is believed that it only comes from an unstable statute law."[39] I believe that the legitimacy of copyright and the legitimacy of the fair use system are issues in two domains of discourse. The establishment of the former does not lead to the establishment of the latter. In fact, under the author's original right recognition criteria "sweat of the brow", the conclusion may be reversed if Locke's theory on labor is used to demonstrate the legitimacy of the fair use system.

1.2.2 Economic Analysis

Economic theory analyzes the legitimacy of the copyright law from two stages. One stage is the period before the creative behavior. The impact of the copyright system on the author is studies. In this stage, if there is no protection for the creative activity, the author will not be motivated sufficiently to innovate, especially when the cost of creative behavior is high without a reward, while the cost of copying directly is low. The other stage is the after-the-fact perspective, that is, when the work has been created. How will infinite copying behaviors influence the social welfare?[40] In the intellectual property system, the rewards of the use and dissemination of works protected by the copyright are more uncertain than those of patents and trademarks. We often see some low-budget movies turn out to be blockbusters, and movies with huge investment are disappointing in box office. Therefore, the "production of knowledge" is full of uncertainty in terms of input and output.

In the economic view of intellectual property, there is a seemingly self-contradictory phenomenon that intellectual property is an incentive, or an opportunity to gain benefits in the market. It is this incentive that induces people to engage in creative behavior that is beneficial to social production. However, the above condition is often not, or only partially, realized, because the holder of intellectual property is given the right to prevent others from accessing this information. Therefore, this kind of inventive for production may hinder the purpose of protection of copyright law, i.e., the spread of knowledge. The system that aims to encourage the creation of new knowledge may be counterproductive in practice.[41] Therefore, in designing the copyright system from the economic perspective, the primary task of cost and profit calculation is to discuss how to reconcile the contradiction between the protection of rights and the obstacles to knowledge dissemination, so as to balance the interests of both.

When creators lose their private funding or other forms of investment, the only way that can guarantee their benefits is by legal protection, with the rights subject

---

[39] Patterson and Lindberg [10].

[40] Zhu [25], p. 35.

[41] Drahos [17], p. 134.

14 1 Theoretical Basis for the Rights Limitation System

and the disseminating entity relying on the transaction with consumers. Unlike most other goods and services that can be traded, a creative work can be used by an unlimited number of people, and the work itself is not consumed. This means that, in general, when one work is disseminated to a wide range of public, the marginal cost of dissemination approaches zero.

1.2.2.1 Transaction Cost Theory

In *The Problem of Social Cost* published in 1960, Ronald Coase points out that any transaction and system has cost. When the transaction cost is too high, both sides of the transaction will choose other ways to help bring about the transaction.[42] "If market transactions were costless, all that matters (questions of equity apart) is that the rights of the various parties should be well-defined and the results of legal actions easy to forecast. But as we have seen, the situation is quite different when market transactions are so costly as to make it difficult to change the arrangement of rights established by the law. In such cases, the courts directly influence economic activity. It would therefore seem desirable that the courts should understand the economic consequences of their decisions and should, insofar as this is possible without creating too much uncertainty about the legal position itself, take these consequences into account when making their decisions. Even when it is possible to change the legal delimitation of rights through market transactions, it is obviously desirable to reduce the need for such transactions and thus reduce the employment of resources in carrying them out."[43]

In 1982, Wendy Gordon proposed that the application of the fair use doctrine is based on market failure. Under the inherent economic logic, the fair use defense in the copyright system is the way to correct the obstacles in copyright related transactions. When the obstacles in the market are so serious as to hinder sales, license and other forms of use can be mutually agreed, and free copying may be permitted.[44] Fair use is a "normal market reaction".[45] If there are factors that hinder market transactions, but the use behavior will not affect the interests of the original rights holder but will facilitate the dissemination of the original work, the purpose of the copyright law to create incentives will not be undermined due to the grant of fair use. Gordon gives three elements of the test for determining fair use: first, in the transaction, the costs of locating and bargaining with each other is prohibitively high; second, whether the use of the work is beneficial to the society; and third, the use behavior would not substantially injure the incentive intended for the rights holder.[46]

This theory is actually an expanded and principled Coase Theorem. Based on this theory, the doctrine of fair use "redistributes" ownership as efficiently as possible to

---

[42] Coase [26].

[43] See Footnote 42.

[44] Gordon and Bone [27].

[45] Dowell [28].

[46] Gordon [29].

1.2 Arguments on the Legitimacy of the Fair Use System

minimize the excessively high transaction costs in the market, the negative consequences of efficiency. The fair use defense allows the bypassing of situation when the transaction costs exceed the residual value of the transaction in the actual market transaction, and believes that under the above circumstances, the direct use of copyrights protected works is a legitimate market reaction. This theory therefore removes barriers of excessively high transaction costs and allows more effective redistribution of resources.[47] Market failure refers to the situation in which the market cannot effectively distribute goods and services. Under the premise of the monopoly nature of copyright, without the protection provided by the fair use system, the public may either do not use the right or use it directly (infringing use) because of the high transaction costs due to the paying of remuneration to the copyright owner. The applying of the transaction cost analysis method to the fair use system focuses on the circumstance where excessively high transaction cost, impairs reaching of the voluntary license agreement and results in market failure.[48]

For the user of the work, once the cost paid to the author or the right owner is less than the benefits obtained from its use behavior, the user will proactively find the rights holder to obtain authorization. If the cost paid to the author or the right owner outweighs the benefits obtained from its use behavior, the fair use system exempts the user from obtaining authorization because of trade imbalance. The "market failure" theory usually occurs in circumstance where the copyright owner and user have to pay costs in order to reach the license agreement. When the costs are too high, the final transaction will not be achieved. Market transactions are not or cannot be completed for some reasons. The traditional theory holds that because of the transaction cost, the authors are required to pay too much for the use of right works. There is a trading environment for this theory. When no new technology or method is used, the rights holder and user of the work are largely in an information asymmetry position. For example, in the process of teaching, teachers need to use different theories or doctrines to complete the teaching process in the process of preparing the lectures. Taking a law class as an example, the content prepared by the teacher may involve natural law theory, empirical law theory, natural school, and empirical school. It is impossible for a teacher to break away from theories or doctrines to introduce different views to students by re-creation. There will always be contents from a work of a jurist or a judge. If all such uses are subject to the permission of the author or the rights holder, it will be difficult for teachers to teach, students to learn, and people who write books to spread their thoughts.

1.2.2.2 Incentive and Innovation

Information circulation path and breadth can solve contradiction between inventive and uneven exchange. When consumers go to grocery stores to buy their turkeys for Thanksgiving dinner, they may be disappointed that the price of turkey is as high as

---

[47] Depooter and Parisi [30].

[48] Feng [31].

it is. At the same time, when farmers bring to market turkeys they have raised, they wish the price of turkey were even higher. These views are not surprising. Buyers always want to pay less, and sellers always want to get paid more. But is there a "right price" for turkey from the standpoint of society as a whole? We know that the price of turkey adjusts to ensure that the quantity of turkey supplied equals the quantity of turkey demanded. But at this equilibrium, is the quantity of turkey produced and consumed too small, too large, or just right? The equilibrium of supply and demand in a market maximizes the total benefits received by buyers and sellers. In a particular sense, the best one is that it maximizes the total welfare of turkey consumers and turkey producers.

Quoted from *Principles of Economics* by Mankiw

Copyright holders might, therefore, find it in their self-interest, ex ante, to limit copyright protection. To the extent that a later author is free to borrow material from an earlier one, the later author's cost of expression is reduced; and, from an ex ante viewpoint, every author is both an earlier author from whom a later author might want to borrow material and the later author himself. In the former role, he desires maximum copyright protection for works he creates; in the latter, he prefers minimum protection for works created earlier by others. In principle, there is a level of copyright protection that balances these two competing interests optimally.

Quoted from *Economic Analysis of Copyright Law* by William M. Landes, and Richard A. Posner

(1) Incentive and innovation

The design of the copyright system seems to be a process of finding a balance between the supply and demand of "turkey". With the development of society, how this property system should be designed to not only provide necessary inventive for innovation, but also enable the works to be used by as many people as possible. Meanwhile, how this system can be designed to suppress free riders.

The connotation of inventive is, the core of the copyright system is to protect authors' rights, and the establishment of the author's core position helps encourage the authors to innovate. The status of works being the object of right with property right nature should be established first. After a work is created, the value of its thoughts and content need be realized by the dissemination of the work. The impact of works on culture, art, science and academics exercise is realized by continuous disseminating the copies of the work. In the traditional circulation environment of works, the inventive function of copyright is reflected in the author's ability to sell copies of his works to the public in exchange for gains and returns. Copyright laws give authors a range of property rights to ensure returns when the author commercializes his works. This is also the basis for encouraging originality and the development of the cultural industries, and guaranteeing the commercial circulation of works.

The connotation of access is to enable the public to obtain and use ideas and expressions in protected works. "The public access the author's expression in the work. By access to the author's expression, the public can further access the author's thoughts." The creation of any work is a process of "taking from the people and

1.2 Arguments on the Legitimacy of the Fair Use System

returning to the people." Anyone can legally obtain and use the work, absorb the knowledge, understand author's thoughts, and even lay the foundation for their own innovation. As a mechanism to balance the interests of all parties, the copyrights limitation system contributes greatly to benefits of users. Manfred Rehbinder believes that all intellectual achievements are part of the country's cultural resources, and the public hopes to enjoy these cultural resources as unrestricted as possible; excessive monopoly of intellectual property is contrary to the public interests. Therefore, in establishing the copyright system, it is necessary to consider how to balance authors' interests with public interests.[49] The relationship between inventive and access is one reason that causes conflicts of interests. The rights holder relies on the monopoly right granted by the system to guarantee the value of the work recovered from the market. However, the dominant position of the rights holder may lead the user to finally give up paying high consideration. "Without monopoly, the production of information cannot be encouraged. With a legal monopoly, there will not be enough information to be accessed by the public." Therefore, it is necessary to find the balance between incentive and access mechanisms to break the institutional dilemma caused by excessive expansion of rights. The balance between incentive and access can be achieved on three levels. The first level is the most basic level of balance, that is, the optimal balance between the inventive to the creator inventive and use by the consumer. This is the balance between effective production and effective consumption. The second level is the balance between rights holders of the original work and users who use the protected work to re-create. The third level is a balance among all entities appeared during technological innovation. Under this new environment, with creation and circulation of the works forming a new interest chain, we need to discuss how to rearrange the status of each subject in the system to achieve a balance.[50]

(2)   Fair use based on price theory

The cost transaction analysis method is based on neoclassical economics. It assumes that the boundary for property rights can be determined and identified, but this is not true. On the basis of transaction cost theory, Belgian scholars further discuss relationship between fair use and copyright protection using the value theory.[51] The equilibrium value theory represented by the British economist Marshall says that equilibrium price refers to the price of a commodity when the demand price and the supply price are consistent, that is, the price at the time when a commodity's the market demand curve meet the market supply curve. In the case of demand being a constant value, the increase in supply will cause shift of the supply curve to the right, which will lower the equilibrium price and increase the equilibrium quantity. Likewise, the reduction of supply will cause the shift of the supply curve to the left, which will raise the equilibrium price and the decrease the equilibrium quantity. The system of limitation on copyright is a means of using the law to get the equilibrium

---

[49] Rehbinder [32].

[50] Zhu [25].

[51] See Footnote 47.

price, and restricting the excessive monopoly of the rights holder. Thus, the system is a kind of benefits for users.

Under the background of reform brought about by new technologies, the doctrine of fair use is seriously impacted under the dissemination of information when strictly obeying the laws and regulations of copyright law. When the use behavior under the new technology is contrary to the position of the copyright owner, the scope of fair use need to be redefined. The popularity of the Internet and the advancement of information dissemination technology have created a new interests relationship. Fair use will become an outdated system. The one-click technology in the information age provides an effective dissemination environment for rights holders and users. The Internet provides rights holders with an opportunity to clearly know the number of use and dissemination of their works. They use the way of digital charging to eliminate transaction costs under the traditional licensing system. Therefore, the traditional doctrine of fair use will become meaningless. Under digital environment, self-regulation of prices will allow the trading of protected works at a more reasonable price.

1.2.3 Constitutional Analysis

Dutch scholar Hugenholtz believes that the establishment of copyright limitations and exceptions in the copyright system is mainly based on the following three reasons. First, the limitations on copyright reflect the respect for the basic rights of citizens, including freedom of speech, freedom of the press, and freedom of information. Second, limitations on private right contribute to the development of public interests in libraries, museums, educational institutions, etc., and ensure citizens' right to education. Third, the limitations on copyright are used to solve the market failure problem in economics.[52]

1.2.3.1 The Balance Between Public Interests and Personal Interests

According to some studies, "public interests" originates from Rome and means interests of the majority and common interests. The public interests are initially used on nations. Some believe that public interests and personal interests are two opposite concepts, and that the two concepts have a long-term relationship of trading off and taking turns. They also believe that the two are not independent separately. In addition to being able to become one another under certain circumstances, the two are more often compatible. That is, the realizing public interests can help with the improving of personal interests. As Montesquieu states, "the public interests include all personal interests. The personal interests put the public interests first." No point

---

[52] Hugenholtz [33]; quoted from Wang [34].

1.2 Arguments on the Legitimacy of the Fair Use System

of view can accurately define public interests. As it is an abstract concept, which makes all viewpoints seem justified.

When discussing the conflict and balance between public interests and personal interests, the focus is to study how to evaluate the personal interests. There are several understandings on personal interests. Some view it as pure economic interests, some view it as the sum of economic interests and personality interests, and some other view it as personality interests that be achieved by economic interests. Scholar Wei Jingzhu summarizes the content of copyright public interests as follows. First, according to the requirement that the content of public interests must be legitimate and reasonable, the public interest goal of the copyright law to promote the orderly prosperity and development of science and culture reflects the pursuit of the copyright law to achieve public order, efficiency, and benefits in the social, cultural, and economic fields. Second, as the legal system is most closely linked to human thoughts and social information, promoting the free flow of ideas and information is embodied in the copyright law. Therefore, the copyright law manifests itself as a time-limited right, and reserves space for restricting rights in the media dominated by public institutions. Third, the public interests in copyright law also reflect the basic democracy and cultural rights of the public, which are manifested in freedom of speech, freedom of information, freedom of self-learning and self-development, social ethics, and reasonable handling of the interests of vulnerable groups.[53]

In the copyright law, fair use for the purpose of public interests generally apply to use for the purpose of: (1) education,[54] although in recent years this purpose of use behavior has gradually been excluded from the traditional scope of fair use, such as the German Act on Copyright and Related Rights, which adds the content of license terms, and in Canadian Copyright Act, which has more detailed provisions on the fair use of data browsing during the studying via the Internet.[55] (2) Criticism and commentary. For instance, Chinese Copyright Law provides that "appropriate quotation from a published work in one's own work for the purposes of introduction to, or comments on, a work, or demonstration of a point", and Italian Copyright Law provides that "for the purposes of comment or discussion, fragments or parts of

---

[53] Wei [35].

[54] For example, in Article 22, Paragraph 1(6) of the Copyright Law of the People's Republic of China, "translation or reproduction in a small quantity of copies, of a published work for use by teachers or scientific researchers, in classroom teaching or scientific research…".

[55] Article 46, Paragraph 1, of the German Act on Copyright and Related Rights: Reproduction, distribution and making works available to the public shall be permissible after publication where limited parts of works, of small-scale literary works and of musical works, individual artistic works or individual photographs are incorporated in a collection which combines the works of a considerable number of authors and is intended, by its nature, exclusively for use during religious ceremonies. According to its characteristics, only for schools, non-profit training or further education institutions, or classroom teaching in practicing education institutions, or churches, this law allows it to be copied, disseminated and publicly provided. (The following limitations were added on January 1, 2008). When the classroom teaching is publicly available, it should obtain permission from the rights holder. The Amendments to Canadian Copyright Law stipulates that educational institutions can use copyrighted materials online and that the fair use can be applied only if the student destroys the copy of the materials within 30 days after the final course assessment.

20 1 Theoretical Basis for the Rights Limitation System

the work may be excerpted, quoted or reproduced and communicated to the public within the scope of the above purposes, which, however, must not compete with the economic use rights of the work"[56]; and (3) personal use (including private copying), such as "use of a published work for the purposes of the user's own private study, research or self-entertainment" in Chinese Copyright Law,[57] and other provisions such as Article 13 of the Japanese Copyright Law, Article 68 of the Italian Copyright Law, and Article 53 of the German Act on Copyright and Related Rights.

The fair use behaviors based on the public interests are mostly manifested in the use for the purposes of "education" and "research". The Berne Convention provides that "It shall be a matter for legislation in the countries of the Union, and for special agreements existing or to be concluded between them, to permit the utilization, to the extent justified by the purpose, of literary or artistic works by way of illustration in publications, broadcasts or sound or visual recordings for teaching, provided such utilization is compatible with fair practice." (Paragraph 2 of Article 10). Meanwhile, "It shall be a matter for legislation in the countries of the Union to permit the reproduction of such works in certain special cases, provided that such reproduction does not conflict with a normal exploitation of the work and does not unreasonably prejudice the legitimate interests of the author." (Paragraph 2 of Article 9). The WIPO Copyright Treaty (WCT) also reiterated that the protection of the author should be limited for the public interests, and the limitations have been restricted to the purpose of education, research and access to information. Maintaining a balance between the rights of authors and general public is secondary in a treaty.[58] It is necessary to emphasize that the main purpose of the treaty is to protect the rights of authors. This idea is also reflected in deciding how the concept of "information" acquired based on public interest should be limited. Therefore, in Paragraph 2 of Article 10 of the Berne Convention, the scope of the information referred to in the Convention is specified, that is, "other forms such as music, film or literature, appreciated regardless of the purpose for the news report, or even obtained online, or included in a database does not constitute a definition of 'information'."[59] The US Copyright Law also excludes the applying of the fair use doctrine on the use of film, drama, or fiction, especially when the use involves the use of the general or entire story line and development of the original with its expression, points of suspense and build up to climax.[60]

1.2.3.2 Tragedy of the Anticommons and Fair Use Doctrine

As a public resource, knowledge can cause different social effects due to different interest choice of the legal system. The establishment of the copyright system can

---

[56] Article 70, Paragraph 1 of the Italian Copyright Law, revised from April 9, 2003.

[57] Article 22, Paragraph 1(1) of the Copyright Law of the People's Republic of China.

[58] Reinbert and von Lewinski [36], p. 31.

[59] Goutal, The WIPO Treaty of 20 December 1996 and the French Conception of Authors' Rights (2001), 187 RIDA 66, quoted from Reinbert and von Lewinski [36], p. 34.

[60] Columbia Pictures Corp. v. National Broadcasting Co., F. Supp. 348 354 (SD Cal. 1955).

1.2 Arguments on the Legitimacy of the Fair Use System

help avoid the phenomenon of "Tragedy of the Commons", which is discussed in this book from the perspective of influences to public interests.

The concept of "tragedy of the commons" comes from the work of Garrett Hardin, the Tragedy of the Commons. He mentions that "as a rational person, every shepherd wants to maximize his own yields", and a tragedy occurs when the shepherd increases the number of sheep in order to increase the yields, because this will eventually lead to the overuse of grassland. He describes that under the circumstance that privilege is given to multiple users to use a given resource without monitoring and constraining their use by way of limiting cost efficiency,[61] the tragedy of fragile resource being overused will occur. Conversely, when multiple owners have the rights to exclude others from using a scarce resource and no one has the right to enforce so, the resource will not be fully utilized. This is *Tragedy of the Anticommons.*

Anticommons is a concept that has been gradually accepted by legal scholars and economics. Michelman proposed this concept in an article on morality, economics and property law in 1982, arguing that since there is public property, "anti-public property" should also exist. Professor Heller further explained the theory of *Tragedy of the Anticommons* in 1998. He pointed out that contrary to the problems caused by the excessive use of resources in the *Tragedy of the Commons*, it was because there were too many rights holders. These rights holders interfered with each other's use of resources. As a result, resources cannot be fully utilized or even stay idle, and this harms the public interests. Both are problems caused by failing to handle the relationship between private property rights and public property rights.[62] In the case of the intellectual property system, *Tragedy of the Anticommons* refers to the excessive monopoly of rights holders, which hinders the sharing of resources among rights holders, and will eventually harm social benefits due to these resources being underutilized. Fair use can seek a balance between *Tragedy of the Commons* and *Tragedy of the Anticommons*, and can both guarantee the legitimate interests of rights holders and provide a way to effectively use knowledge resources.

1.2.3.3 Embodiment of "Freedom of Speech"

In *Twin Peak Prods, v. Publication Intern'l*, the United States Court of Appeals for the Second Circuit stated that "maybe except for some special circumstances, 'in the lawsuit of copyright…, the fair use doctrine encompasses all claims of first amendment in the copyright field'".[63]

In the United States, the fair use doctrine is a benchmark that maintains the balance between the First Amendment to the Constitution (Amendment I) and the Copyright Act. On the one hand, the purpose of the Copyright Act is to protect the interests

---

[61] Tragedy of the Commons [EB/OL]. [2012-09-10]. http://wild.mbalib.com/wild/tragedy%20of%20the%20commons.

[62] Tragedy of the Anticommons [EB/OL] [2012-09-10]. http://zh.wikipedia.org/wild/tragedy%20of%20the%20anticommons.

[63] Twin Peak Prods, v. Publication Intern'l, 996 F. 2d 1366, 1378 (2d Cir. 1993).

derived from works; on the other hand, Amendment I ensures unstoppable flow of information. Therefore, the doctrine of fair use requires a careful and delicate balance of interests; "on the one hand, the author and the inventor control and use the interests of their works and inventions; on the other hand, it is opposite to the free-flowing competitive interests of ideas, information and trade in society."[64] Monopolistic right to expression is contrary to the freedom of expression protected by the Amendment I. The construction of copyright law should be designed for the purpose that it should achieve, that is, to promoting creative achievement.

In 2000, the German Federal Constitutional Court overturned a judgment of the Bavarian High Court made in 1998 in accordance with the constitutional provisions on the protection of artistic freedom.[65] The Federal Constitutional Court held that used of Berto Brecht's work in a script called *Measures 1956* by Heiner Muller, a playwright and poet, was protected by the Basic Law. The judgment of State Court, according to the German Act on Copyright and Related Rights,[66] violated the freedom of art provided in the first sentence in Paragraph 3 of Article 5 of the German Basic Law. Further, based on the political attitude and expression of the author presented in the script, the judgment of the State Court also violated the freedom of expression provided in Paragraph 1 of Article 5 of German Basic Law.[67] Here, the fair use system finds a solution to the conflicts between the upper level law and the lower level law. In this sense, the fair use system breaks away from the framework of the private rights system of copyright and assumes some of the functions of public law.

1.2.4 Sociological Analysis

Private copying and innovative reuse are the main kinds of use that fall within the realm of fair use. Both of them accompany people's acquisition of knowledge and innovation, and are not products of the copyright system. The reason that we discuss the legitimacy of the copyright system from the above perspective is that, in the

---

[64] Jonathan [37].

[65] Bverf G, 1 BvR 825/98 vom 29. 6. 2000, AbsatzNr. (1-33), see Shan and Liu [38].

[66] The judgment was based on Article 97 of the German Act on Copyright and Related Rights in combination with Article 15, Paragraph 1, Paragraph 16, and Paragraph 17, and the court held that the defendant did not quote the citation in its own way. "Freedom of citation should serve the freedom to argue with the minds of others, and can also be carried out by restating the individual passages of the works protected by different authors to clearly illustrate the political, scientific or ideological trends. However, citations are only allowed as an example of the citation's own discourse." See Shan and Liu [38].

[67] Article 5 of the German Basic Law: (1) Every person shall have the right freely to express and disseminate his opinions in speech, writing and pictures and to inform himself without hindrance from generally accessible sources. Freedom of the press and freedom of reporting by means of broadcasts and films shall be guaranteed. There shall be no censorship. (2) These rights shall find their limits in the provisions of general laws, in provisions for the protection of young persons and in the right to personal honour. (3) Arts and sciences, research and teaching shall be free. The freedom of teaching shall not release any person from allegiance to the constitution.

1.2 Arguments on the Legitimacy of the Fair Use System

history of human civilization, the birth of a work is not necessarily an innovation. In the theological era especially, creative behavior was only defined as the behavior of recording God's will and communicating to the public by a specific person, with the inspiration of creation from the guidance of God. Even in the Renaissance period when scholars and artists gradually began to pay attention to the pursuit and affirmation of self, the borrowing of predecessors' thoughts and works was inevitable. From the birth of a man, his' understanding of the world, mastering of language, and formation of ideas are all from experiences, and the creation of works is also based on experiences. Therefore, from the beginning of the establishment of the intellectual property system, scholars have been keen to justify the establishment of this right. After nearly 300 years of establishment and improvement, the rights and status of intellectual property are now deeply rooted in the hearts of the people, and scholars are now trying to find a breakthrough in the nature of private right-based copyright for the original creation form of "fair use".

1.2.4.1 Legally Recognized Factual Behavior Forced by Dynamics of Internal Demand of Social Exchange

With regard to "interests", Marx wrote that, "everything that people strive for is related to their interests."[68] Further, in social life, the main way for people to realize their own interests is through exchange. In the process of exchange, a new balance of interests is achieved. "All contact between people depends on the model of giving and returning being equivalent. The equivalents of countless gifts and performance can be implemented. In all legal forms of economic exchange, all agreements involving established services to be determined, and all the obligations of legal relationship, the law regulations enforce and guarantee the mutuality of service to the return service. Without this mutuality, the social equilibrium and cohesion will cease to exist."[69] The circulation of knowledge realizes the society's communication function. In the social relationship established by people, their interests are expressed, and their desires are fulfilled. The public feature of knowledge is mainly manifested in the following two aspects. First, knowledge is a tool for human communication and people with the same knowledge background can communicate with each other. Second, the spread of knowledge directly affects the development of science and culture. Taking books as an example, being able to read and to communicate in writing is no longer confined to ancient Greek aristocrats or medieval popes. The spread of knowledge has improved people's understanding of their rights. Through the exchange of knowledge, people receive education, which enables most people to strive to raise from the lowest needs in Maslow's hierarchy of to the highest needs, self-actualization. Therefore, people realize a part of their needs through the exchange of knowledge.

Any attempt to evaluate the behavior based on the foreseeable outcome of a particular activity is contrary to the role played by the opinion of whether the relevant

---

[68] Marx [39].

[69] See Sociology by Georg Simmel quoted from Blau [40].

behavior should be endorsed in the formation of a comprehensive order.[70] Most human behaviors are governed by rules that limit the behavior within allowable range—these rules generally refer only to certain types of behaviors, and ignore their predictable and specific outcomes. We should combine legal norms with social activities to understand "the law in daily life" from the context of society, culture, economy, and politics, rather than narrow the scope of research into the law (articles of law, legal precedents or judgments) itself, namely, "law in the books", with a final aim to stimulate social analysis of law.

"The extreme importance of spontaneous order or the rule of law is based on the fact that it expands the possibility of peaceful coexistence for mutual interests. These people are not small groups with common interests, and they do not have to obey a particular superior. The order comes from gradual growth. It adopts certain rules as the basis, and these rules are established because the groups that follow these rules are more successful. Before people realize their existence or understand their operational mechanisms, these orders have been formed."[71] In the copyright system, the behavior of fair use has always been there, as can be seen from the laws of continental countries in Europe, which provides the specific circumstances under which fair use can be applied. Many rights limitations and exceptions provided by law sometimes seem unnecessary. For example, imitating, a copying behavior, is a kind of fair use that does not require exemption by law. In the case of knowledge, a product that fulfill rights by dissemination, it is impossible to achieve absolute control of knowledge in the sense of real rights. Therefore, more attention should be paid to transactions rather than ownership in designing the system.

The concepts of "fair prices", "fair reward" or "fair income distribution" have been thought over by philosophers for two thousand years. Finally, fair prices and wages are defined as prices and wages formed spontaneously in markets without fraud, violence and privileges. This conforms to the theory of fair behavior, which says that there is no fair state, but only fair behavior. Whatever results caused by the impartial behavior of all relevant individuals are fair, because they are the results of people's own choice. Since fair reward or distribution is only meaningful within an organization whose members are managed by a common target system, it does not make sense in an economic or spontaneous order without such a common goal.[72]

The legitimacy of intellectual property can be explained within the framework of the personality theory. This theory provides a single person with a single or particularly beneficial mechanism for self-time, individual expression, respect and government of men. When the personality theory is used in the field of intellectual property, it can be used in a self-consistent manner. The reason why thought belongs to its creator is that thought is the manifestation of the personality and self of the creator.[73]

The creation of the author, the appreciation by the user, the recreation based on new inspiration, and the feelings that connect the works of different periods of time,

---

[70] von Hayek [41], p. 327.

[71] von Hayek [41], p. 346.

[72] von Hayek [41], p. 353.

[73] Li [19], pp. 208–209.

1.2 Arguments on the Legitimacy of the Fair Use System

these show the exploration and sharing of knowledge by human beings, and are the most basic social communication. An author's sense of satisfaction depends on the action of others. If a person only feels satisfied when enjoying food, collective endorsement to a certain privilege is enough to explain the legitimacy.

1.2.4.2 Interplay of Law and Cultural Development

The evolution of biology depends on the inheritance and mutation of genes; the evolution of culture depends on the sharing of information. Speech is the most basic and primitive communication tool of human beings. When there is no way to put down things in writing, human beings can only communicate orally. Therefore, the evolution of culture was extremely slow then. Recording is an accelerator for the evolution of human civilization. Civilization develops with the evolving of the means of recording, for instance, the development of language symbols from animal bones to books, art symbols from rock carvings to church murals, music from tribal sacrificial ceremonies to records in households, and drama from open-air stage to cinema. From the fixation of "knowledge" to how to spread "knowledge", it is not only a study of human culture, but also a study of the object of rights (i.e., works) and the content of rights (i.e., reproduction) in copyright which law cares about.

Fair use, as an important part of the copyright law, and a system that restricts the economic interests of rights holders, has played a role in the development of culture. At the same time, the development of culture also has an impact on the determination of "the boundary of copyright, a private right."

1. Cultural modernization

The transformation of culture from traditional to modern is mainly characterized in medialization and commodification.

(1) Cultural medialization

British scholar Thompson believes that a prominent feature of modern culture is mediatization, that is, "the symbolic form of modern society has become more and more mediatized by the mechanisms and institutions of mass propagation."[74] In the entire cultural field, from the creation and circulation of works to their impact on the ideas and ways of life of the public, each aspect has the characteristic of "mass propagation". The ideology with this characteristic is gradually formed and developed. Eventually, a modernized culture is formed.

The grand narrative of cultural transformation can be summarized in three stages.[75]

First, the rise of industrial capitalism in Europe and other places was accompanied by the decline of religious beliefs and customs popular in pre-industrial societies.

---

[74] Thompson [42], p. 83.

[75] Thompson [42], p. 85.

The development of industrial capitalism in economic activities was accompanied by the secularization of beliefs and customs and the rationalization of social life in the cultural field.

Second, the decline of religions and witchcraft laid the foundation for the rise of the secular belief system or "ideology". The ideology had nothing to do with mobilizing remediation actions and was independent of the value or existence of the afterlife. The religion and deepened understanding of the pre-industrial society was rooted in social collectivism and replaced by the reality inspired by the secular belief system.

Third, these developments promoted the rise of the "ideology era", which reached a peak in the late 19th and early twentieth centuries represented by the fund revolution, and ended in the 1950s and 1960s by works.

The development of mass propagation provides new opportunities for the generation and dissemination of images and information. By relying on technical media for transmission, images and information are provided to a wide range of audiences in terms of time and space. The images and expression of media information develop after television is developed and can be received and perceived by a large number of individuals at geographically dispersed locations.

(2) Cultural commercialization

Horkheimer and Adorno pay particular attention to the rise of what they call "cultural industry," which has led to the increasing commodification of cultural forms. Therefore, the early Frankfurt school theorists emphasized the importance of mass media development. They used the term "cultural industry" to refer to the commercialization of culture brought about by the rise of the entertainment industry in Europe and the United States in the late 19th and early twentieth centuries. They used examples including movies, radio, television, pop music, magazines and newspapers. The cultural products of these industries are designed and manufactured for the purpose of accumulating capital and realizing profits. Cultural products are not produced spontaneously by people, but are tailored to group consumption. This process has led to the shrinking ability of the people to think and act in a critical and funded manner.[76]

A major trend in the creative behavior is that the author has added consideration to the market demand in their creative process. When British literature became popular in the early twentieth century, a professor of literature at Oxford University even felt sick at his own "useless novel".[77] The contemplation and appreciation of art works are replaced by commodity exchanges, and their value is first and foremost based on its exchange value, not its inherent aesthetic nature. The products of the cultural industry are very different from traditional works of art. Before the eighteenth century, art can maintain certain independency outside the market. This is due to a patron system that protects artists from the needs to earn a life. This independency allows works of art to maintain a certain distance from reality, express suffering and

---

[76] See Thompson [42], pp. 107–120.

[77] See Eagleton [43].

1.2 Arguments on the Legitimacy of the Fair Use System

contradictions, and have their understandings of a better life. However, with art being increasingly applying the logic of commodity production and exchange, the critical potential inherent in the purposelessness of traditional art forms is lost.

In the traditional society, the notion that emphasizes the spontaneity, autonomy and independence of human beings is cultivated by philosophy and religion. Restricted by the differentiation in education and classes, this kind of philosophical thinking are only limited within a small scope, i.e., in aristocratic families. On the contrary, the modernity of culture is formed along with the appearing of large-size industrial organizations, and more people involved in this culture. When the characteristics of many individuals are immerged into the whole society and culture, the individual does not stand in the opposite of the traditional ideas, but affects modern culture together with traditional ideas.[78] The western cultural heritage and schools have always been using "classicalism" as a benchmark. For example, "Gothic" which started from the twelfth century and lasted until the sixteenth century, originally meant "not yet reaching the classical standard"; "Baroque", a popular architectural styles popular in the seventeenth-eighteenth centuries, means strange and weird, as compared to classicism. Classicalists illustrate the characteristics of "Baroque" as deviating from the classical form with their own deviant expressions. Western history of art always involves a fixed classical principle and various deviations. Of the styles and historical periods that every beginner has learned, including Classicism, Romanesque, Gothic, Renaissance, Mannerism, Baroque, Rococo, Neoclassicism, and Romanticism, all of them fall into two categories, classical and non-classical.

With the development of digital technology, the characteristics of cultural commodification is becoming more and more prominent. For example, the success of a movie or a literary work depends largely on box-office revenues or sales, which are the effect of commercialization operation. This reflects the public's preferences. Further, it encourages more capitals to be invested in "creation" that meets the needs of the public for high commercial returns. At the same time, the integration by big data with the support of Internet technology has further contributed to the formation of a commoditized cultural atmosphere, which is both the reason for the formation of data thinking and a result of the effective use of big data.[79] Nowadays, people find that the news they receives, the articles that they read in their mobile phones, the videos that are interspersed in the titles, etc., are not as broad or boundless as people thought in the early days of the Internet, but are more and more concentrated or even narrowed. This is the result of targeted launching in the era of big data, and a means of commercial marketing. Therefore, the commercialization trend of culture is becoming more and more prominent.

2. Interplay of copyright and modern culture

The progress of science and the development of technology have given birth to the copyright system and even the entire intellectual property system. The intellectual property system has been established to "promote and encourage innovation", and

---

[78] See Thompson [42].

[79] Wang [44].

28   1 Theoretical Basis for the Rights Limitation System

has contributed to the scientific progress and the innovations of knowledge. If the commercialization of modern culture drives the rights holders by greater interests, the mediatization of culture brings about a wider demand for the public to access knowledge. The cultural trend of mass propagation itself has also improved the public's democratic awareness of free access to knowledge.

Establishing a system that restricts the copyright, an absolute right, is an adaptive tool that is required to be used in the modern cultural environment. It guarantees people's freedom to access "knowledge" in the process of cultural propagation. Benjamin believes that in the era of mechanical reproduction, although art has lost the "spirit" under the traditional technical conditions, the new technology has caused the development of culture in the direction of "democratization."[80] In the fields related to education, academic research and criticism, people no longer believe in authority, and the meaning of culture is no longer unique. The greatest characteristic of democratization is that people can express their opinions anytime and anywhere. With the emerging of self-media in the Internet environment, people can express themselves through text, pictures, audio and video, or any combination of them, and spread the same in a variety of ways.

The copyright system plays a very important role in the development of culture. Another interpretation of "encouraging innovation" in intellectual property is to limit "copying". This limitation has far more profound significance on culture than on economic benefits. American scholar An Shoulian believes that the only purpose for China's efforts to protect intellectual property before the twentieth century was to maintain the imperial power.[81] This phenomenon coincides with the original intention of the European censorship on books and newspapers from the end of the fifteenth century to the early eighteenth century.[82] Both of them are aimed at maintaining the feudal rules.

Today, China is facing a complex environment. From the economic perspective, social development in China is in an era composed of rural economic society, industrial economic society and post-industrial economic society. Corresponding, in China's social activities, and even the entire Chinese cultural tradition, China is deeply affected by the Confucianism. Some parts of the Confucian culture have universal value, while some are the feudal culture. The intellectual property system is a system that challenges "authority" and rewards "innovation". People need to pay for the copying behavior. Therefore, the copyright system itself will have a revolutionary impact on the development of Chinese culture.

References

1. Li Mingde, Xu Chao. Copyright Law [M]. Beijing: Law Press, 2003: 110

---

[80] Benjamin [45].

[81] Shoulian [46].

[82] Shen [47].

References

2. Liu Chuntian. Intellectual Property Laws [M]. 4th ed. Beijing: China Renmin University Press, 2009: 127
3. Sun Shan. Legal Interests Not yet Raised to Rights: Definition for the Nature of Fair Use and Legislative Advices [J]. Intellectual Property, 2010, 3
4. Dong Binghe. Fair Use: Exception of Copyright or Users Rights [J]. Studies in Law and Business, 1998, 3
5. Wu Handong. Thoughts on Fair Use System from the View of Civil Law [J]. Jurists Review, 1996, 1 (6): 54–62
6. Wu Handong. Analysis of the Legal Value of the Fair Use System [J]. Science of Law: Journal of Northwest University of Political Science and Law, 1996 (3): 30–38
7. Wu Handong. Research on Copyright Fair Use [M]. Beijing: China University of Political Science and Law Press, 2005: 131
8. Zhang Ming Kai. Criminal Law [M]. 3rd edition. Beijing: Law Press, 2007
9. Chang Lin, Feng Yangyong. On the Defect and Perfection of the Exemption of Tort Liability [J]. Journal of North University of China: Social Science Edition, 2006, 22 (4)
10. Patterson LR, Lindberg S W. The Nature of Copyright: A Law of User's right [M]. Athens: the University of Georgia Press, 1991
11. Rosenoer Jonathan, Cyber Law [M]. Zhang Gaotong, etc. trans. Beijing: China University of Political Science and Law Press, 2003: 49
12. Zhang Mingkai. New Criminal Law and Infringement of Legal Interests [J]. Chinese Journal of Law, 2000 (1)
13. Stephen Holmes, Cass R. Sunstein. The Cost of Rights: Why Liberty Depends on Taxes [M]. Bi Jingyue, Trans. Beijing: Peking University Press, 2011
14. Yu Jiucang. Instrumentalism of Intellectual Property Rights: Reading Drahos "A Philosophy of Intellectual Property" [M]//Liu Chuntian. Chinese Intellectual Property Review (Volume 1). Beijing: The Commercial Press, 2002
15. Cao Yixin, Qiu Lisheng, Liu Hua, Ren Yan. Economic Analysis of Intellectual Property Protection System: Essentials of Software Knowledge Property [M]. Beijing: China Social Sciences Press, 2008: 22–23
16. Locke. Second Treatise of Government [M]. Ye Qifang, Qi Junong, Trans. Beijing: The Commercial Press, 1964: 19
17. Peter Drahos. A Philosophy of Intellectual Property [M]. Zhou Lin, Trans. Beijing: The Commercial Press, 2008
18. James Tully: A Discourse on Property, Cambridge, 1980
19. Li Yufeng. Law Triggered by the Guns: Study on the Chinese Copyright History [M]. Beijing: Intellectual Property Publishing House, 2006
20. Rose M. Authors and Owners [M]. Harvard University Press, 1993: 27
21. Alexander Passerin d' Entrbves. Natural Law: An Introduction to Legal Philosophy [M]. Li Rizhang, et al. Beijing: New Star Press, 2008: 60
22. Zhou Changzhong. Cultural Spirit of Western Science [M]. Shanghai: Shanghai People's Publishing House, 1995: 46
23. The Albert Einstein Collection (Volume 1) [M]. Beijing: The Commercial Press, 2009
24. Xu Peng. Copyright Fair Use System under the Horizon of the Development of Communication Technology [D]. Changchun: Jilin University, 2011
25. Zhu Hui. Incentive and Access: The Economic Research on the Copyright System [M]. Hangzhou: Zhejiang University Press, 2009
26. Ronald Coase. The Problem of Social Cost [J]. Journal of Law and Economics, 1960, 3
27. Gordon W. J., Bone R. G. Encyclopedia of law and economics [M]. Northampton, MA, 2000
28. Dowell J. Bytes and pieces: Fragmented copies, licensing, and fair use in a digital world [J]. California Law Review, 1998, 86 (4): 843
29. Gordon W J. Fair Use as Market Failure: A Structural and Economic Analysis of the Betamax Case and its Predecessors [J]. Colum. L. Rew. 1982, 82: 1614–1622
30. Depooter B, Parisi F. Fair Use and Copyright Protection: A Price Theory Explanation [J]. International Review of Law & Economics, 2002

31. Feng Xiaoqing. On Fair use of Copyright and Its Economic Analysis [J]. Journal of Gansu Political Science and Law Institute, 2007 (4)
32. Manfred Rehbinder. Copyright Law [M]. Zhang Enmin, Trans. Beijing: Law Press, 2005: 62
33. Hugenholtz B. The Future of Copyright in a Digital Environment [M]. Kluwer Law International, 1996: 94
34. Wang Qing. Comparative Study on Regime of Limitations of Copyright [M]. Beijing: People's Publishing House, 2007: 40
35. Wei Jingzhu. Research on Public Interests in Copyright System [M]. Guangzhou: Sun Yat-sen University Press, 2011: 55–68
36. Jorge Reinbert, Silke von Lewinski. The WIPO Treaties on Copyright [M]. Wan Yong, Xiang Jing, Trans. Beijing: China Renmin University Press, 2008
37. Rosenoer Jonathan, Cyber Law: The Law of the Internet [M]. Zhang Gaotong, et al. Beijing: China University of Political Science and Law Press, 2003: 53
38. Shan Xiaoguang, Liu Xiaohai. Judgment of the Federal Constitutional Court of Germany on Artistic Freedom Stipulated in the Constitution and Reasonable Quotation Relationship Stipulated in the Copyright Law [J]. Intellectual Property Right Law Research, 2004, 1
39. Marx, Engels. Collected Works of Marx and Engels (Volume 1) [M]. The Bureau for the Compilation and Translation of Works of Marx, Engels, Lenin and Stalin Under the Central Committee of the Communist Party of China, Trans. Beijing: People's Publishing House, 1972: 82
40. Peter Michael Blau. Exchange and Power in Social Life [M]. Li Guowu, Trans. Beijing: The Commercial Press, 2008
41. Friedrich von Hayek. Hayek Selections [M].2nd edition. Feng Keli, Trans. Nanjing: Jiangsu People's Publishing House, 2007
42. John B. Thompson. Ideology and Modern Culture [M]. Gao Xian, Trans. Nanjing: Yilin Press, 2005
43. Terry Eagleton. Literary Criticism and Theory in the Twentieth Century [M]. Wu Xiaoming, Trans. Beijing: Peking University Press, 2007
44. Wang Hansheng. Data Thinking [M]. Beijing: China Renmin University Press, 2017
45. Walter Benjamin. The Work of Art in the Age of Its Technological Reproducibility [M]. Hu Bushi, Trans. Hangzhou: Zhejiang Literature & Art Publishing House, 2005
46. An Shoulian, Intellectual Property Rights or Ideological Control: A Culture Probe into Traditional Law in Ancient China [M]//Liang Zhiping, Trans. Liu Chuntian. Chinese Intellectual Property Review: Volume 1. Beijing: The Commercial Press, 2006
47. Shen Guchao. Rise and Fall of the European Press Censorship [M]. Nanjing: Nanjing University Press, 1999

Chapter 2
Legislative Status of the Fair Use System

There are four ways to express the concept of "fair use" in foreign copyright laws and theoretical researches[1]: first, "fair use": which is used in the Copyright Act of the United States, the Philippine intellectual property law, and the Tunisia model copyright law; second, "free use": a term used in the Italian copyright law and the Berne Convention; third, "fair dealing": a term used in English law, which is used in countries and regions that are deeply influenced by English law, such as the United Kingdom, Australia, New Zealand, Canada, Hong Kong, etc.; and fourth, "bright use" or "fair use": these terms are used in Japan, whose Copyright Law is deeply influenced by the German Act on Copyright and Related Rights.[2] Different expressions in different countries and regions reflect different understandings and limitations of the rights limitation system of copyright.

Unlike other limitations in the copyright system, the fair use exception is not a typed right. This exception is open-ended, with the boundary not clearly defined. First, the explanation of "fair" in fair use is illustrated by examples. Second, in the Copyright Act of the United States, the fair use system is only an explanation with a guiding nature, rather than specific limitations; while some other countries enumerate in their statutes the situations that fair use applies, which gives the judge a high degree of discretion.[3] Common law countries uses "factorialism" as the basis to judge the specific behaviors in specific cases, while the civil law countries based on "regularism" clearly define the specific behaviors of fair use, "users can clearly predict the consequences of their behavioral when they use works".[4]

---

[1] Wang [1].

[2] Handa and Takatani [2].

[3] Armstrong [3].

[4] Liu [4].

© Intellectual Property Publishing House 2021
S. Liu, *Rights Limitation in Digital Age*,
https://doi.org/10.1007/978-981-16-4380-4_2

2.1 Case Law Countries

The concept of fair use was originally found in a series of cases from 1740 to 1839. The British judges created a series of rules in handling specific cases. These rules allow other authors to use a work without having to obtain the original author's consent.[5]

2.1.1 United States

(1) Doctrine of fair use

The US Copyright Act of 1976 is the result of negotiations among interests groups related to copyrights. The legal language of this law itself is influenced by authors, publishers, and other economic interests. The final statute reflects the needs of all parties.[6] However, this law does not involve the interests expressed by the end consumers. The evolving path of the US copyright system is like a process in which the rights holders strive to incorporate the resources in the public domain into their protection. The rights holders' seem to be never satisfied with their monopoly on public resources. Further, after resources are included into their scope of protection, they are divided among related interests groups.

The US Copyright Act provide factors that can be considered in regard to the application rules of the fair use system; while in actual judicial activities, cases are taken as fundamental rules and judging criteria.

In the Copyright Act of the United States, "fair use" is considered a doctrine, as "it allows for some kind of reproduction of the expressive component of a copyrighted work (i.e., the component actually protected by copyright), even if the right holder does not authorize the behavior of copying, and the behavior of copying is not deemed as an infringement". This doctrine is codified as Article 107 of the Copyright Act of the United States, which states that the fair use of a copyrighted work, including such use by reproduction in copies or phonorecords or by any other means specified by that section, for purposes such as criticism, comment, news reporting, teaching (including multiple copies for classroom use), scholarship, or research, is not an infringement of copyright. In determining whether the use made of a work in any particular case is a fair use, the factors to be considered shall include (1) the purpose and character of the use, including whether such use is of a commercial nature or is for nonprofit educational purposes; (2) the nature of the copyrighted work; (3) the amount and substantiality of the portion used in relation to the copyrighted work as a whole; and (4) the effect of the use upon the potential market for or value of the copyrighted work. The fact that a work is unpublished shall not itself bar a finding of fair use if such finding is made upon consideration of all the above factors.

---

[5] Zwart [5].

[6] Maggs [6].

2.1 Case Law Countries

As a principled clause, the concept of "fair use" in US Copyright Act is not clear. In *Gray v. Russell* and *Folsom v. Marsh*, Judge Joseph Story of the United States applies the basic notion of fair use. These two cases are regarded as the blueprint for the fair use system in the US Copyright Act.[7] In 1839, in *Gray v. Russell*, Judge Joseph Story held that in judging whether the use of other people's works constitutes a copyright infringement, the focus is not the quantity of the part that is cited, but the value of that part.[8] However, in 1841, in *Folsom v. Marsh*, the judge ruled that Folsom, who published a number of copies of the George Washington Letters, won the case because the defendant Marsh had quoted as many as 350 pages from Washington letters in a 866-page book he published. Since then, the concept of "fair use" has been constantly challenged by these precedents.

In *Campbell v. Scott* in 1842, the judge stipulated the basic obligations of a user in using others' works, and held that fair use is not applicable to simple and direct use of other people's works without explanation or comment. He also held that in deciding whether use of a copyrighted work by a third party is justifiable and whether it constitutes a copyright infringement, the decision should not be based on whether there is an infringement on the basis of the use of the content of the work, in form or in substance, but shall be first judge whether the use behavior damages the copyright owner's rights on his works. If the use caused damages, it should be regarded as a constituent element of infringement.[9]

In *Scott V. Stamford* in 1867, the judge made an exclusionary statement about the purpose of using someone else's works, i.e., the use shall not have profit motives and purposes of impairing the value and market of the original work. *Lawrence v. Dana* in 1869 and *Simms v. Stanton* in 1896 both mention that the premise of fair use is that the use of expressions that have been fixed in the works, and ideas, concepts, styles, etc. are not protected.[10]

In 1869, the term "fair use" is first used in *Lawrence v. Dana*. But in the copyright law of 1909 and for a long time thereafter, this term was not explained in a code, as it is difficult to determine what kind of use behavior can be considered as "fair".[11] In the Copyright Act of 1976, there was clear statement on fair use, which says that for the purposes of criticism, comment, news reporting, teaching, academics, and research, copyrighted works can be entirely reproduced.

(2) Challenges to the fair use doctrine due to technology advancement

With the advancement of technology, there are more and more ways to copy protected works. The following cases reflect the changes in the fair use doctrine in the US jurisprudence.

In 1973, in *Williams & Wilkins Co. v. The United States*, the copyright holder sued libraries with a large number of books and magazines for allowing other libraries

---

[7] Wu [7].

[8] 10 F. Cas. 1035 C. C. D. Mass. (1839).

[9] Cai [8].

[10] Xu [9].

[11] Henslee [10].

and research institutions to copy copyrighted articles using copiers. The focus of the dispute was on whether the copying behavior of libraries is fair use.[12] Although the court finally determined that the libraries' behavior of providing copying services to the readers is fair use, the exception to the prohibition of mass copying was added to Article 108 of the subsequent US Copyright Act. After this case, in 1978, under the advocacy of the US Congress, the United States established a non-profit copyright clearing center, which is a collective management organization of copyright. Through the intermediary service of the organization, right holders obtained a certain amount of copying license fee, which basically solved the problem of obtaining profits from copyright use.[13] This kind of compensation for copyright owners essentially excludes the copying behavior of the library from the fair use system, and defines it as statutory license. This is determined by the progress of the copying technology, because the interests of copyright owners have been substantially damaged with the inventing of photocopiers. As right holders cannot control the copying behavior of the public by counting the number of "replications" in a way same as calculating the sales of the books, the statutory licensing method becomes a solution.

In 1982, in *Encyclopedia Britannica Educational Corp v. Crooks*, the judge held that the school's systematic and consistent recording of television programs and repeated use thereof in the teaching process were not fair use.[14] In 1976, the White House report on copyright law made detailed descriptions of the behavior of recording programs for teaching purposes. The act of recording a program and playing it in the classroom is an act of use for educational purposes in fair use. This report suggests that the retention of the recorded program may be limited to 45 days. Beyond this time limit, the doctrine of fair use is no longer applicable. In addition, the video playback behavior used in teaching should also meet the following conditions: the recording behavior is based on the teacher's teaching requirements; due to the limitations of the TV program playing time, the program used for teaching has to be recorded; the number of time for playback after recording should be limited to one time; playing the recorded program needs to be closely connected with the teaching activity, otherwise it will no longer be a fair use behavior.[15] In 1984, in *Sony v. Universal Studio*, the court ruled that "noncommercial home recording of television broadcasts for the purpose of 'time-shifting' was fair use".[16] This is a lawsuit arising from private copying. Universal Studios and Disney Pictures believed that the technology to manufacture and sell Sony's Bebamax recorders actually helps consumers achieve infringement. In the Audio Home Recording Act of 1992 enacted by the United States, private recordings were exempted from bearing legal liabilities. According to this Act, no one may file a lawsuit for infringement of copyright against non-profit private recordings; copyright compensation was set up, and manufacturers

---

[12] 487 F.2d 1345 (Ct. Cl. 1973).

[13] Zhangjin [11], pp. 54–55.

[14] 542 F. Supp. 1156 (W. D. N. Y. 1982).

[15] Guidelines for Off-the-Air Recording of Broadcast Programming for Educational Purposes, Cong. Rec. @ E4751, October 14, 1981.

[16] 464 U. S. 417 (1984).

2.1 Case Law Countries

who manufacture blank digital recording equipment and media must pay royalties to compensate the losses that copyright owners may suffer as a result of home recording; and digital recording equipment sold in the United States must be equipped with a system that prevents digital files from being copied multiple times.[17] In this Act, the definition of "non-profit" private recording behavior is based on technical conditions. The number of private copies, the quality of personal recorded programs, and the extent to which private copying may spread are not sufficient to cause substantial damage for the right owners' selling market at the time. As far as the speed and status quo of technology development are concerned, non-profit private copying is no longer an excuse for the fair use exemption. The hardware system of knowledge dissemination has been overwhelmingly changed. Thus, private copying can only be judged in a very specific situation. However, how to define a behavior remains an issue.

In 1986, in *Maxtone-Graham, v. Burtchaell,*[18] of the 37,000 words in the first chapter of Burtchaell's work, about 7000 words were quoted from a work by Maxtone-Graham. In the quotation, there was a paragraph which is an interview record on "wrong pregnancy". Burtchaell's work has a total of 325 pages and the first chapter is about 60 pages. The court held that fair use shall apply in this case, as the defendant only extracted about 4.3% of the plaintiff's work, and had given the source of the reference regarding this section.[19] In the process of using the plaintiff's work, the defendant had made efforts to discuss the licensing issue with the plaintiff and had obtained the plaintiff's initial approval. However, the plaintiff filed an infringement lawsuit on the reference in the published book. Based on the four factors of the fair use doctrine, the defendant's citation was determined as fair use.

The following conclusions can be drawn regarding the rule for the application of the fair use doctrine: the defendant's citation behavior does not lead the consumer to view the defendant's work as a substitute for the plaintiff's work; the defendant's reference to the plaintiff's work is for commentary purpose, and is not direct use for commercial purposes. In recent years, this rule has also been used in *Browne v. McCain,* a lawsuit filed during the 2008 US presidential election regarding the use of Browne's musical works in the background of McCain's campaign commercial.[20] The court determined that it's a fair use behavior, and that the commercial used multiple pieces of music and obtained the consent of the original authors. The main reason is that the purpose of use in the new work is different from the original work, and thus does not affect the use of the original work and the market.

The legitimacy of fair use in the *Campbell v. Acuff—Rose Music* case means that even if the user has applied for authorization but is denied, the use of the work is still legal. Cases of parody and satire continue to challenge the scope and boundaries of fair use, and the application of fair use is becoming much stricter. The rules

---

[17] Zhangjin [11], p. 56.

[18] 803 F. 2d 1253 (1986).

[19] See Footnote 18.

[20] Case No. CV 08-05334 (2008).

36   2 Legislative Status of the Fair Use System

established in specific cases in the United States are a result of coordinating the interests of all parties to achieve some kind of balance.

2.1.2 United Kingdom

The origin of the use of the word "dealing" in the UK is clearly related to the original formulation of copyright law as a trade rule. After nearly two centuries of development in UK, the fair dealing doctrine first appeared in the U.K. Copyright Act in 1911.[21] Article 19 of the current UK Copyright Law stipulates that any unauthorized performance, showing or playing of work in public is prohibited and is not judged by commercial purposes, including classes, speeches, lectures, etc. Article 21 stipulates that making adaptation or act done in relation to adaptation is prohibited.

The limitations on rights by the provisions of the UK Copyright Act are smaller in scope than that in the Copyright Act of the United States, and the application of fair use is more stringent. The main considerations in the UK Copyright Law are as follows[22]:

1. The nature of the work: if an unpublished work or a confidential work is used, the defendant will lose the case.
2. The way to obtain the work: if the work is leaked or plagiarized, any use of the work is unlikely to be a fair use.
3. The amount of using of the work: the amount used shall be small, and such use shall be beneficial to a fair use; but in some cases, the use of an entire work may also be fair, for example, if the work is short.
4. Whether the way of use changes the form of the original work: the greater the change, the greater the possibility of being a fair dealing.[23]
5. Commercial benefit: if the use of the original work makes the user actually obtain economic benefits, this will weigh against the user regarding his purpose of use, that is, it will not be determined as fair use, except for certain researches for the purpose of public interests.[24]
6. The motivation of the use behavior: the court adopts the target criteria and considers whether there is malicious or altruistic motive.
7. Consequences of the use: this factor is about the impact of the new works on the original works in the market, especially in a competitive environment. If a new work substitutes the original, this use should not be considered as fair dealing.
8. The purpose of use: the provisions on fair dealing enumerate the purpose of use, including research or private study, criticism or comment, reporting of current

---

[21] UK Copyright Act, 1911, Section 2 (1) (i).

[22] Agostino [12].

[23] Vaver [13]. Quoted from Agostino [12].

[24] *Newspaper Licensing Agency Ltd. v. Marks & Spencer Plc*, [1999] RPC 536, [1999] E.M.L.R.369 (CA) [Marks & Spencer] from Agostino [12].

2.1 Case Law Countries

events.[25] Fair dealing in the UK Copyright Law has sparked many academic debates. Some scholars believe it does not involve any substantive principle doctrine, and contains too many obstacles.[26] When judging whether a dealing is fair, it is difficult to achieve the "fair" side by all the above factors, which makes legal practices difficult.

(1) Determination of the purpose of use in fair dealing

In determining the purpose of use, the first factor that needs to be considered is whether the use is for research or private study purposes. The British courts believe that research and private study must be for a non-commercial purpose. "Regulations on fair use, for temporary reproductions, are limited to individual research and study, that is, a use behavior limited to home is allowed."[27]

However, some commentators in the UK believe that the criteria for judging whether the use of a database is fair dealing is open to discussion. If the use of database is for business training, such use would constitute research or private study. However, it is still difficult to define what is "commercial". One key factor may be that the research need not be private. Another factor to be considered is the effect of the number of copies on the market, because such copying results in a large amount of resources that are transmitted and protected. In addition, the use for this purpose is not applicable to broadcasting, recording and movies.

The second factor is whether the use is for criticism or commentary purposes. In this regard, it should be determined first whether the user obtained the works through legal means. If not, such use is not fair use. In *Sillitoe v. McGraw-Hill Book Company*,[28] the court ruled that a large number of references and abridgement of the original work led the consumer to read the defendant's comments instead of purchasing the original work. Thus, the use behavior affected the selling of the original work in the market. The act of citation, abridgement or commentary that affects the sale of the original work does not fall into fair use. In *Newspapers Group v. News Group Ltd*,[29] The Sun, the defendant, published letters from the Duke of Windsor and the Duchess, and the rights holders of these letters were Daily Mail, the plaintiff. If the defendant only intended to write this as news, there is no need

---

[25] The third chapter of the UK Copyright Law provides for exceptions to the use of copyright, Article 28A provides for the production of temporary reproductions, Article 29 provides for research and personal study, and Article 30 provides for criticism, evaluation and news reporting. Article 31 describes the accompanying use of copyright works, and in the subsequent articles of the rules, detailed provisions are made for the specific circumstances of various fair use actions, including those related to "visual impairment"; Provisions of use for educational purposes (Articles 32–36); Provisions of use for libraries and archives (Articles 37–44); Provisions related to Public Administration (Articles 45–50); Provisions related to Computer Software (No. 50 Article); Provisions related to design (Articles 51–53); Provisions related to fonts (Articles 54–55); Article 56 on works in electronic form; and other rules.

[26] Craig [14]. Quoted from Agostino [12].

[27] Quoted from Agostino [12].

[28] [1983] F. S. R. 545.

[29] [1986] R. P. C. 515.

to publish these letters. Thus, the purpose for the defendant to publish these letters is to attract readers, and the motivation of its citation is for "commercial use". The court ruled that the defendant was infringing and fair dealing could not be applied on the grounds of news reporting. The reason is that "the defendant's motivation is to use the work consciously and obtain economic benefits, but not for a commentary purpose."

The third factor is whether the use is for the purpose of current-events reporting, or news reporting. The purpose of the current-events reporting is generally interpreted as news reporting. In the *Pro Sieben Media v. Carlton Television* case,[30] the application of fair use regarding news reporting is more rigorous. Sieben produced an interview program featuring an interview with a pregnant woman of octuplets, and Carlton copied the 30-min show and spliced it into a 30-s show in its reporting. Sieben believed that the use of Carlton infringes on its copyright, while Carlton argued that its action was fair dealing permitted by law, as this copying was performed for a report on current events. However, Sieben believes that they paid the interviewee for the show, and Carlton's news report may become a substitute for the whole program, thereby damaging its economic interests.

Justice Walker believes that criticism or commentary is not limited to a concept. Comments on social or moral issues in current events can also apply fair dealing. The act of making a report by excerpting part of the original program is in line with the characteristics of comment, so it is a fair dealing behavior.

(2)   The dealing must be fair

Hubbard and another v. Vosper and another[31] has an important place in the UK Copyright Act. It established a testing standard of fairness to prove that the defendant's use is fair. In Article 6 of the UK Copyright Act of 1956, the Hubbard case explained the concept of "fairness". A former church member of Cyril's family wrote a book regarding the church founded by Lafayette Ronald Hubbard on the basis of the contents of a book. The dispute is whether the use by Vosper violates Hubbard's copyright. Lord Denning said that the question of whether a dealing is fair depend on the facts and degree, and all the circumstances of a particular case must be fully considered. However, it is impossible to accurately define what is "fair dealing". It must be a matter of degree. First, the quantity and scope of the quotations and extracts, as well as the use of substantive content must be considered. Is it because they are used too much or too long to apply the fair use doctrine? Second, you must also consider the use made of them. If they are to be published as a comment, in the sense of criticism or comment, this may be a fair dealing. It may be unfair if they are used to convey the same information for the purpose of becoming the author's competitor. Finally, it is important to consider the issue of the proportion of citations. To quote a piece of content and to attach a short sentence may be fair. However, short citations and long comments may be unfair, then other considerations may be involved. After all, what is said and done is different. It must be an impression on a specific problem.

---

[30] [1999] 1 W. L. R. 605.

[31] [1972] 2 Q. B.

2.1 Case Law Countries 39

Therefore, the court must weigh the scope and proportion of the quotation, as well as the position of the quotation in the original work. Even if a whole work is used (for example, for competition purpose), it may be protected by fair dealing. Since the 1998 Human Rights Act, it is of utmost importance that courts need to consider the public interest flexibly.

(3) Factors to be considered

In *Ashdown v. Telegraph Group Ltd*,[32] the court established a hierarchy of factors to determine fair dealing, which include:

(a) Whether the use of the alleged infringement may have a market substitution for the use of the work by the copyright owner: if the behavior of fair dealing causes the new work to obtain a status that can replace the original work, fair dealing is "destined to be inapplicable."

(b) Whether the work has been published or exposed to the public before publication: if not, the fair dealing doctrine should not be used, especially when the works are obtained through some illegal means.

(c) The extent of use and the importance of the part of use: the method of verification is to examine whether the extent of the defendant's use is necessary to achieve its relevant purpose.

Other factors that need to be considered include:

(d) The motives of the alleged infringer: for example, whether the use uses fair dealing as an excuse;

(e) The purpose of use, i.e. whether the use is necessary or not;

(f) If the work being used has not been published, whether the act of copying is obtained by the defendant through stealing or in other ways: published or unpublished works may have opposite effects.

In the UK, the impact of the market is the most important factor, and the market affects the author's right to remuneration. This requires the court to further emphasis on this factor.

2.1.3 Canada

The provisions of the Copyright Law of Canada related to the fair use system were initially similar to those of the United Kingdom, and were later influenced by the US Copyright Act. Canada includes a fair use doctrine in its Copyright Act. The provisions stipulate that fair use is limited to the use of copyrighted works for research and private study, criticism or commentary, and news reporting. Only when these behaviors meet one of the enumerated purposes, can they be fair use. Because "if the purpose of use is not in the circumstances stipulated by the Copyright Law, the

---

[32] Laddie et al. [15].

court cannot use the fair use exemption."[33] After Canada incorporated the concept of "user right" into the core concepts of the copyright law system, a new balance in the copyright law is struck between the promotion of the public interest and the rewards provided to the creators. The understanding of fair use turns from negatively viewing the act of fair use as an exception to understanding it as a user right that is a part of the Copyright Act. Of course, the Copyright Act of Canada imposes very specific rules on the application of fair use to avoid the abuse of the system and the injury to the interests of the copyright owners.

The application of digital technology also poses a challenge in measuring the appropriateness of fair use. "In the digital world, the copyright 'balance' is no longer adequately served by application of the concept of reproduction"[34] As can be seen, the impact of digital technology subverts the "copying" behavior, a core concept in the entire copyright system. The traditional balance of interests has been broken. Under what circumstances should the user with browsing behavior in the digital environment offer the author a corresponding return is still the core issue that should be addressed in the digital environment.

The case filed by Commerce Clearing House (CCH Canadian Ltd), Canada Law Book Inc.,Thomson Canada Ltd. and many other law publishers against the Law Society of Upper Canada ("Law Society") ("CCH case") has an important impact on the influence and development of Copyright Act of Canada. Since 1845, Society has been running a large library which was one of the libraries in Canada with the most rich resource of legal literature. The library provides both copy services to readers, and file transfer services to readers by sending copies to the requester by mail or fax. In 1993, the law publishers ("CCH") jointly filed an infringement lawsuit against the Law Society, claiming that the library infringed the copyrights of multiple works published by CCH', and applied for an injunction prohibiting infringement by the library. The Law Society denied the alleged infringement, and believed that for research purposes, a single copy of the judgments of a res judicata, case summaries, laws and regulations, or a limited portion of the text of a treaty made by library staff and autonomous copying by the user were all within the scope of "fair use" as stipulated in the Copyright Act of Canada. The Federal Court of Appeal finally ruled that CCH's claim for copyright in all the works involved was supported. However, the library developed a reasonable resource access policy, which allows copying of works within this policy framework. Thus, user right in the Canadian Copyright Act is clarified.

---

[33] In the CCH case, Judge Linden explained the important influence of the closed-end enumeration purpose of the Copyright Law. Quoted from Gast [16].

[34] Litman [17], referring to Gast [16].

2.2 Civil Law Countries

In many countries in the world, regulations on the fair use system combine principle and enumeration. For example, the Korean Copyright Law adopts such a legislative model, i.e., it both enumerates the various situations that works are allowed to be used, and specifies a series of factors that can be used as a reference when judging whether a particular situation constitutes a fair use.[35] However, there is a view that in most countries where the limitations on and exceptions to copyright are stipulated by enumeration, the courts adopt a relatively closed and cautious attitude towards fair use. In actual cases, the rationality of other behaviors beyond the categories listed in the legislation is rarely considered.[36] This phenomenon explains the status of the fair use system in the current judicial environment.

2.2.1 Germany

Section 6 of the German Act on Copyright and Related Rights involves the limitations on copyright, which regulates the application of fair use in a strict manner. For example, Article 47 is related to the broadcasting behavior for schools, which is similar to that of the United States. Specifically, Article 47stipulates that:

1. Schools, teacher training and further training institutions may make individual copies of works to be used as part of a school broadcast by transferring the works to video or audio recording mediums. The same shall apply to youth welfare institutions and state image archives or comparable institutions under public ownership.
2. The video or audio recording mediums may only be used for teaching purposes. They must be deleted at the latest at the end of the academic year following the transmission of the school broadcast, unless the author has been paid equitable remuneration.

The German Act on Copyright and Related Rights stipulates different scopes and methods of free reference of different works. In order to promote the development of science, the law not only allows quoting small passages in other people's works, but also allows copying the entire article in scientific papers, the entire poem in cultural history books, the artistic artwork in art history books, and description of technology in technical works. This is the so-called "big citation". At the same time, it also defines the "small citation", namely, to promote the cultural and musical creation, only a fragment of literary and art works can be quoted, and the user cannot only use the quotation without giving any explanation.[37]

---

[35] Song [18].

[36] Cohen et al. [19].

[37] Shan and Liu [20].

2.2.2 Japan

Same as the legislation of the typical civil law countries, Japan's current copyright law adopts the method of enumeration for its limitations on copyright. That is, it enumerates the specific circumstances according to the purpose of use and the status of use. However, in recent years, due to the development of internet technologies and the diversification of communication methods, Japan had been planning to amend its copyright limitations in the near future, and intends to adopt the form of Copyright Act of the United States. In 2009, the amendment to the Japanese Copyright Law was centered on expanding the scope of copyright and at the same time imposing stricter limitations on the rights.

First, it expanded the scope of rights in the reproduction for the purpose of private use, the right of reproduction has effect on the infringed digital recording or video recording received through public communication automatically on knowing the facts.

Second, the scope of rights is further restricted on the following:

1. In the National Library of Congress, substituting the original copy of the library materials for public use is considered as being within the limits deemed necessary, and electronic records can be produced.
2. Usage by persons who are engaged in the welfare of people with visual or hearing impairments, those who are prescribed by the government, for the purpose of visual or hearing impaired persons, is considered as being within the limits deemed necessary. Reproduction can be made by changing literature into sound or changing sound into words.
3. If the owner of the original art or photography product does not infringe the transfer right or the right to lease of the copyright owner and intends to transfer the original, it may be copied or distributed to the public for the purpose of the transfer application.
4. In the business, the person who conducts the activity by using the automatic public communication device for others for communication, in order to prevent the transmission of the work from being hindered when the automatic public communication device is failed, can record the work that can be propagated to the medium within the limits deemed necessary.
5. Internet information retrieval service operators may, within the limits deemed necessary, record the work that can be propagated on the recording medium and use the record and the source identification mark together for automatic public communication.
6. In order to analyze the work information with a computer, it can be recorded in the recording medium if it is considered necessary.
7. When the work is used on a computer, in order that the information can be processed smoothly and efficiently, the work can be recorded on a computer recording medium as far as it is considered necessary.
8. When the whereabouts of the copyright owner or the related right holder of the copyright are unknown, the person who proposes the application for the custom

2.2 Civil Law Countries

of the Cultural Office may, in the case of depositing the amount of the guarantee amount specified by the head of the Cultural Office, use the work according to the use method in the application ruling before the ruling result is come out.

9. For the copyright register, the publication right register, and register of related right of copyright, all or part of it can be made with disk.[38]

This amendment to the Japanese Copyright Law complies with the challenges on the legal system brought about by technological development. It adopts a more cautious attitude on the system of limitation on copyright. However, regarding the use of works via computers, the user is given a certain space for copying. Based on public interest considerations, it emphasizes the government's functions, and reflects that the administrative agency has a complete plan for dealing with orphan works.

2.3 International Treaties

The Berne Convention for the Protection of Literary and Artistic Works ("Berne Convention") explicitly stipulates the copyright limitations and exceptions. Member States are permitted to establish limitations and exceptions on the following acts:

1. As a general provision for exceptions, Article 9.2 recites: "It shall be a matter for legislation in the countries of the Union to permit the reproduction of such works in certain special cases, provided that such reproduction does not conflict with a normal exploitation of the work and does not unreasonably prejudice the legitimate interests of the author."
2. Article 2bis. 2 provides that: "lectures, addresses and other works of the same nature which are delivered in public may be reproduced by the press, broadcast...";
3. Article 10.1: "It shall be permissible to make quotations from a work which has already been lawfully made available to the public, provided that their making is compatible with fair practice, and their extent does not exceed that justified by the purpose, including quotations from newspaper articles and periodicals in the form of press summaries."
4. Article 10.2: "It shall be a matter for legislation in the countries of the Union, and for special agreements existing or to be concluded between them, to permit the utilization, to the extent justified by the purpose, of literary or artistic works by way of illustration in publications, broadcasts or sound or visual recordings for teaching, provided such utilization is compatible with fair practice."

Article 13 of TRIPS provides for limitations on and exceptions to copyrights: "Members shall confine limitations or exceptions to exclusive rights to certain special cases which do not conflict with a normal exploitation of the work and do not unreasonably prejudice the legitimate interests of the right holder."

---

[38] Yang [21].

The three-step test is a principled description of specific copyright limitations and exceptions. It consists of three elements: "specific description of the application of limitations on rights holders", "the reasons for the existence of exceptions", and "results of the exceptions".

Step 1: Some special circumstances.

"Some special circumstances" should be understood as exceptions that can only occur for a specific purpose of use. "The broad exceptions that cover many objects or methods of use are considered to be inconsistent with this provision. In addition, exceptions should be justified by a well-defined public policy or other special circumstances."[39]

Step 2: Conflict with the normal use of the work.

Whether it is commercial or not is objectively difficult to distinguish, and not every commercial use of the work will cause substantial damage to the right holder. However, when the use situation of fair use competes with the way in which the right holder obtains economic benefits under normal circumstances, a conflict of interest arises,[40] thereby causing damage to the right holder. Therefore, the judgment of normal use should exclude the occurrence of competitive relations.

Step 3: Unreasonable damage to the legitimate interests of the right holder.

When an exception or limitation causes a loss of income for the right holder, such an act is unreasonable, as it would substantially damage to the interests of the right holder.

The WTO Dispute Settlement Team explains the three-step test in the case of the Fairness in Music Licensing (DISPUTE DS160) filed by the European Union in accordance with Article 110(5) on the US Copyright Act, that is:

1. The three-step test is a cumulative condition. A certain behavior must meet all three conditions in order to be considered as meeting the requirements of the three-step test. Violation of any step in the three-step test is a violation of the three-step test;
2. The scope of application of "special circumstance" is quite narrow and must be clearly defined; and
3. Affecting the fair use of a work means that the act has a competitive relationship with the usual way in which the right holder obtains economic benefits from the work.[41]

The application of the three-step test method in judicial practices of the EU countries is quite different. France, Netherlands etc. follow stricter rules of application, while Germany, Spain etc. follow relatively loose standards of application. Such

---

[39] United Nations Conference on Trade and Development [22], p. 172.

[40] United Nations Conference on Trade and Development [22], p. 174.

[41] Yin [23].

2.3 International Treaties

difference corresponds with the copyright limitations jurisprudence of each country. As far as Germany is concerned, its system of rights limitations is more detailed, and the enumeration of circumstances that fair use applies is relatively adequate. Therefore, its application of the three-step test is reflected in a more relaxed manner than France.

There is a debate in the academic world on whether to add the three-step test method to China's copyright law. Some think that the three-step test method differs from the four principles of fair use in that the application conditions of the three-step test itself are harsh and the scope of application of fair use is greatly restricted. Unlike the comprehensive judgment factors adopted by the US doctrine of fair use, the three-step test provides that "as long as one of the step is violated, it constitutes a violation to the three-step test."[42] When the economic interests of the protected work are affected, fair use should not be applied. This makes the fair use system actually invalid and harms the public interest.

The three-step test method and the four principles of fair use are essentially the same. In the process of amending the copyright law in China, we need to consider which method is to be used as the principle clause. For this purpose, the whole framework of the rights limitation system should be taken into consideration. We need to first make clear whether is it plausible for us to enumerate all circumstances for the application of fair use as "detailed" as Germany or Japan does. When the enumerated circumstances can basically meet the needs of judicial practice, we can choose to adopt the four principles of the fair use as a catch-all clause. On the contrary, as the technology continues to evolve, it is difficult for the specific circumstances listed in the law to meet the needs of practice. Thus, a relatively strict criteria for fair use is needed. In addition, since the three-step test establishes a high wall for fair use, it objectively contributes to the development of the statutory licensing system. This not only safeguards the economic interests of the right holders, but also ensures the realization of the public interest.

2.4 Legislation in China

2.4.1 Laws

Article 22 of Chinese Copyright Law stipulates the specific circumstances of fair use.[43] At the same time, the "Three-Step Test" method is embodied in the Regulations

---

[42] See Footnote 41.

[43] In the following cases, a work may be exploited without the permission from, and without payment of remuneration to, the copyright owner, provided that the name of the author and the title of the work are mentioned and the other rights enjoyed by the copyright owner by virtue of this Law are not infringed upon: (1) use of a published work for the purposes of the user's own private study, research or self-entertainment; (2) appropriate quotation from a published work in one's own work for the purposes of introduction of, or comment on, a work, or demonstration of

46   2 Legislative Status of the Fair Use System

for the Implementing of the Copyright Law, with Rule 21 stipulating that: "The use of published works with no need permission from copyright owner by provisions concerned of the Law shall not harm the normal exploitation of the work concerned and shall not unreasonably prejudice the legitimate interests of the copyright owner."

The legislative principle of rights limitation system in Chinese copyright law is based on the "legislation-centered doctrine". Many of its provisions can no longer provide protection on rights of copyright owners under the digital technology. For example, the use for the purpose of self-entertainment is fair use according to the current law. However, this is uncertain, and any use of a protected work may be for self-entertainment. Regarding the circumstance provided by Article 22.2, which says "appropriate quotation from a published work in one's own work for the purposes of introduction of, or comment on, a work, or demonstration of a point", there is neither a provision with principled limitation nor a provision on the degree. Article 22.9 provides that the boundary of fair use is that a performance neither charge from the public nor the pay remuneration to the performers. Such description cannot be equated with commercial use, and is thus flawed. Further, Article22.8 does not limit the number of copies that the library and archive can make. Thus, even if these institutions are capable of purchasing the original works, they may still choose to make reproduction of the original work. This will certainly harm the interest of the right holder. The circumstance provided in Article 22.7, which says "use of a published work by a State organ within the reasonable scope for the purpose of fulfilling its official duties", lacks legal justification. The application of Article 22.5 in real life is also very controversial. News reporting, a text system of modern public affairs, has created the concept of the "public" in the various processes of

---

a point; (3) inevitable reappearance or citation of a published work in newspapers, periodicals, radio stations, television stations or other media for the purpose of reporting current events; (4) reprinting by newspapers or periodicals or other media, or rebroadcasting by radio stations or television stations or other media, of the current event article s on the issues of politics, economy and religion, which have been published by other newspapers, periodicals, radio stations or television stations or other media, except where the author has declared that publication or broadcasting is not permitted; (5) publication in newspapers or periodicals or other media, or broadcasting by radio stations or television stations or other media, of a speech delivered at a public assembly, except where the author has declared that publication or broadcasting is not permitted; (6) translation or reproduction, in a small quality of copies, of a published work for use by teachers or scientific researchers in classroom teaching or scientific research, provided that the translation or reproduction is not published or distributed; (7) use of a published work by a State organ within the reasonable scope for the purpose of fulfilling its official duties; (8) reproduction of a work in its collections by a library, archive, memorial hall, museum, art gallery or similar institution, for the purpose of the display or preservation of a copy of the work; (9) free of charge performance of a published work, that is, with respect to the performance, neither fees are charged from the public nor the remuneration is paid to the performers; (10) copying, drawing, photographing, or video recording of an artistic work located or on display in an outdoor public place; (11) translation of a work published by a Chinese citizen, legal entity or organization, which is created in the Han language (Chinese), into a minority nationality language for publication and distribution within the country; (12) translation of a published work into Braille and publication of the work so translated; the provisions in the preceding paragraph shall be applicable to the limitations on the rights of publishers, performers, producers of sound recordings and video recordings, radio stations and television stations.

2.4 Legislation in China

Western modernization. Today, it has more shifted to the "private life" and "non-news", and expanded from daily political, economic, cultural, public affairs and other reporting areas, such as lifestyle, fashion, tourism, furniture and gardening, leisure and consumption. This further blurs the line between citizens and consumers.[44] Even commentary reporting on current events may be protected by copyright and may not be used in a paid manner.

2.4.2 Cases Involving Fair Use

(1) *He Ping v. Ministry of Education, Examination Center*

In November 2007, the People's Court of Haidian District of Beijing held a trial of the copyright infringement case filed by He Ping, a cartoonist from Jilin City, who claimed that the Examination Center of Ministry of Education infringed the copyright of his works during the 2007 national college entrance examination.

Facts: He Ping created a cartoon named "Fall" in early 2005, and published it on "Satir and Humor". This cartoon won the excellent work prize in the "ManWang Cup" cartoon competition. After the college entrance examination in 2007, He Ping found that the cartoon was used in the essay question of the national college entrance examination. Although revisions were made to the explanatory note and details of the work, the concept and structure remained unchanged. He Ping sent a letter to the Ministry of Education on this usage behavior, but did not receive any response. He Ping then brought a lawsuit against the Ministry of Education, claiming that the defendant had infringed his right to remuneration, right of authorship and right of modification. The defendant admitted that the cartoon used in the college entrance examination was revised from plaintiff's work, but argued that the cartoon used in the essay question of the college entrance examination is different from the original.

The court first determined the nature of the two works. During the court hearing, the court admitted that the two works bear similarities. However, the court held that, cartoon was an art form that combines paintings and explanatory note; by expressing the author's worldviews, it aim to achieve the effect of satire or praising, and provide inspirations and insights. Thus, the court held that although the two cartoon have similarities in composition, character modeling and story design, their meanings are very different, and thus the two works are different; as such difference has exceeded the meaning of the original works and formed a new one, the new work is a derivative work.

According to Article 22 of the Copyright Law of China, "use of a published work by a State organ within the reasonable scope for the purpose of fulfilling its official duties" is a circumstance that constitutes fair use. Thus, such use does not require asking the permission of the copyright owner or payment of remuneration. In this regard, the Examination Center of the Ministry of Education argues that its

---

[44] Hartley [24].

behavior is a fair use of the state organs for the purpose of fulfilling its official duties. Although the Examination Center of the Ministry of Education is not a state organ, its organizing of the college entrance examination is performing a national official conduct. Article 20 of the Education Law of the People's Republic of China stipulates that "The state shall adopt a national examination system of education. The national educational examinations shall be categorized by the department in charge of educational administration under the State Council and be conducted by institutions authorized by the state to organize examinations." According to this provision, the Examination Center of the Ministry of Education accepts the special task of organizing the college entrance examination and higher education self-study exams, and carries out the corresponding official duties such as the paper proposition for college entrance examination. The Examination Center of the Ministry of Education deducted and used the plaintiff's work in the process of organizing the high exam papers. Such conduct falls with the scope of using a published work by a State organ within the reasonable scope for the purpose of fulfilling its official duties, whether it is from the nature of the behavior of organizing the high exam papers by the Examination Center of the Ministry of Education, or the purpose and scope of the use of the works in organizing the high exam papers. Thus, according to Article 22.1 (7) of the Copyright Law of China, there is no need to ask for permission or pay remuneration.

However, another focus of the case is whether the moral rights of the comic book authors should be recognized, namely, whether the source of the work should be clarified in the college entrance examination. The court held that copyright is a private right, but it plays a role in balancing the public interest. The fair use system is an exception to and limitation on the rights of the copyright owner on the premise that the copyright owner's interest is protected. The purpose is to balance the interests of the copyright owner, the disseminator of the work and the public. Although the Copyright Law of China stipulates the limitations on the fair use, it should be a general principle that allows exceptions under special circumstances subject to objective situations, practical needs or industry practices. For example, Article 19 of the Regulations for the Implementation of the Copyright Law stipulates that "[a]nyone who uses works owned by others shall show clearly name of the author and title of the work; but exceptions exist if involved party has another agreement or can't show clearly due to special character of using the work." The court held that the situation that the cartoon does not have a signature in the essay question of the college entrance examination falls into the above exception.

In the Judgment, the court explained why it is reasonable to not affix the author's name: "1. during the college entrance examination, time is limited and valuable to the examinees. The examinees' attention is also very limited. If the source of the questions is provided with a signature, it will increase the examinees' time to read the information, waste the valuable time of the examinees, and affect the seriousness, standardization and accuracy of the exam. Second, signature on the carton is an useless information for the essay question, and it is appropriate to do so in order to prevent candidates from wasting time and attention on useless information. 3. In similar language examinations at home and abroad, there are situations where cartoons used in essay questions are not affixed with the name of the author. As far

2.4 Legislation in China

as this case is concerned, the Examination Center did not use He Ping's original comic, but a new comic work that has a very different meaning and new idea. The copyright of the work is owned by the editor, even if a signature need to be provided, it is not the name of the plaintiff that shall be signed. Therefore, the conduct of the Examination Center who did not affix the name of the plaintiff to the cartoon used in the essay question of the college entrance examination does not constitute infringement."

In this case, failing to affix the name of authors on the cartoon used in the college entrance examination is an act that ignores the author's moral rights. The following explanations of the court are not reasons to despise the author's moral rights. First, the court held that the examination time is precious and the adding of the author's name will increase the amount of information that examinees need to process; the signature information is contrary to the seriousness of the examination, and is useless information, which will increase the reading burden of the candidates. These reasons are based on value judgment. A signed cartoon work may also bring more ideas to the examinees. At the same time, it has a subtle effect of educating and warning the examinees to respect intellectual property. Second, the court found that in the examination information of domestic and foreign countries, some exams are also not signed. Such kind of reference is not comparable in the case. On the contrary, this reason suggests that it is normal to affix names on the cartoons used in an exam, which is irrelevant to the status of the examinees. Finally, the court held that the cartoon had been adapted and the copyright owner should be the editor. On the one hand, He Ping's status as the right holder of the original work is recognized; on the other hand, the existence of the derivative work is recognized. The unauthorized modification of the original work infringes He Ping's copyright, and not signing the name of the original author is a further infringing act.

The fair use system is concerned not only with "unauthorized, free use", but also respect for the author's moral rights. In this case, even though the organizing of examination is recognized as the performing of official duty by a state organ, and, the original author's authorization cannot be obtained in advance because of the particularity of the exam, the author's moral rights should be respected in strict accordance with the legal provisions on fair use.

(2) Fair use to introduce musical works—*Chen Shaohua v. China Music Copyright Association*

Facts: Chen Shaohua, a singer, had a song named "September 9 Wine", which was popular all over China more than a decade ago. In mid-October 2007, Chen Shaohua sued the China Music Copyright Association ("Music Copyright Association") in the Wuhan Intermediate People's Court, claiming that the Music Copyright Association, which had provided audition service of the clip of the song "September 9 Wine" on its official website without his consent, violated his right to his musical works. Chen claimed damages of about 30,000 yuan.

During the first instance, the Music Copyright Association believed that the purpose for it to provide the clip of the song "September 9 Wine" on its website (signed with Chen Shaohua as the singer) was to introduce the work of the members of the Music Copyright Association. The clip of the song provided to the audience was to identify songs, which is not for commercial purposes. At the same time, the Music Copyright Association believes that the song clip it provided was only 23 s, which is less than 1/10 of the whole song. It was less than the internationally accepted practice of intercepting audition music. It did not bring any economic loss to Chen Shaohua. Therefore, according to the Copyright Law, the act is fair use, and no permission or enumeration was required. However, the plaintiff's lawyer believed that the use of the Music Copyright Association for commercial purposes.

The Wuhan Intermediate People's Court held in the first instance judgment that although the Music Copyright Association was entrusted by the songwriter of the song involved in the case to manage the work, and although the audition of the song clip provided on the website also had the purpose of introducing the song, the playing of the song involved Chen Shaohua's performance and still need to ask for permission. In view of the fact that the song clip played on the website of the Music Copyright Association was only 23 s, and there was no evidence that the Music Copyright Association gained benefits therefrom, the behavior of the Music Copyright Association had limited impact on Chen Shaohua's rights. Therefore, the court determined that the Music Copyright Association should stop using the song "September 9 Wine" sung by Chen Shaohua on the website and should compensate Chen Shaohua for economic losses and reasonable expenses totaling 5900 yuan.

The Music Copyright Association, being unsatisfied with the first instance judgment, appealed to the Higher People's Court of Hubei Province. After the second instance hearing, the Hubei High People's Court held that the Music Copyright Association was a collective management organization of copyright. In addition to the authorization of the copyright owner on the song when Music Copyright Association manages the work of its members, it must also obtain the permission of Chen Shaohua when using the performance of the involved musical work. However, as a rights protection organization, the Music Copyright Association had already fulfilled its duty of due attention and regulating its own behavior, and had took necessary precautions when posting Chen Shaohua's song "September 9 Wine" on its website. Although the behavior of the Music Copyright Association was not a circumstance of fair use as stipulated in the Copyright Law, the "economic loss" claimed by Chen Shaohua was not supported because the harm was minor, and the Music Copyright Association neither directly gain profits from the promotion of the song, nor cause any actual economic loss to Chen Shaohua. In view of the above, the Hubei High People's Court changed the first instance judgment, ruling that the Music Copyright Association compensate Chen Shaohua a reasonable expenditure of 2900 yuan. The litigation fee for the two instances was shared by the Music Copyright Association and Chen Shaohua.

The focus of dispute in this case is whether the audition service of song clip provided by the Music Copyright Association for the promotion of member's works on its website is fair usage. According to the 12 circumstances of fair use in Article 22 of the Copyright Law of China, the Music Copyright Association believed that its behavior is an "appropriate" use behavior in fair use on the grounds of its "introduction and commentary" purposes. The main reason that the judgment by the court of

2.4 Legislation in China

the first instance is not approved is that there is no explicit provision in the law indicating that the use by the Music Copyright Association is fair use. At the same time, it is also because of the drawback for following the "legislation-centered doctrine" in legislative method. Both courts hold that there is no clear provision in the Copyright Law of China regarding the fair use of the rights of performers. They ignore the catch-all clause of the Copyright Law on the fair use system. Article 22 of the Copyright Law clearly stipulates the provisions applicable to the fair use as stipulated in the law "[is] applicable to the rights of publishers, performers, producers of sound recordings and video recordings, radio stations and television stations." However, it is a pity that this clause is not used in judicial practices. However, the second instance court overruled the infringement determination by the first instance court, which follows the principle of copyright limitation to some extent. In order to help the public identify a song, music works must be somewhat reproduced when they are introduced. In this case, whether the reproduction is a circumstance of fair use is analyzed based on the application principles of fair use. First, the use of the work by Music Copyright Association is for the purpose of introducing its member's works, not for commercial purpose; second, the work is a legally published work; third, a reference shorter than 1/10 of the entire work is short and appropriate; and fourth, a musical work that is as short as 23 s is difficult to bring adverse consequence of replacing the original work. In fact, such purpose with an introductory nature is aimed at promoting the work of the right holders and facilitating the obtaining of economic benefits. Further, as this use behavior does not have any negative impact on neighboring rights holders, it should be fair use.

References

1. Wang Qing. Comparative Study on Regime of Limitations of Copyright [M]. Beijing: People's Publishing House, 2007: 163
2. Masafumi Handa, Takao Takatani. Copyright Law 50 Lectures [M]. Wei Qixue, Trans. Beijing: Law Press, 1990: 218
3. Armstrong T K. Digital rights management and the process of fair use [J]. Harvard Journal of Law & Technology, 2006: 30–31
4. Liu Haihong. The Dilemma of Coordination of Copyright Limitation System in EU Network Environment: From the Perspective of the European Court of Justice (ECJ) InfopaqCase [J]. Journal of Henan Institute of Education (Philosophy and Social Sciences), 2011, 2
5. Zwart M D. A historical analysis of the birth of fair dealing and fair use: lessons for the digital age [J]. Intellectual Property Quarterly, 2007
6. Maggs P B. The balance of copyright in the United States of America [J]. American Journal of Comparative Law, 2010
7. Wu Handong. On Fair Use [J]. Jurisprudence Research, 1995 (4): 43–50
8. Cai Huiru. Future Prospect of Copyright: Value Innovation of Fair Use [M]. Taipei: Angle Publishing Co., Ltd., 2007: 66–67
9. Xu Peng. On the fair use of copyright under the vision of communication technology development [D]. Changchun: Jilin University, 2011: 13
10. Henslee W. You can't always get what you want, but if you try sometimes you can steal it and call it Fair Use: A Proposal to Abolish the Fair Use Defense for Music [J]. Catholic University Law Review, 2009, 58 Cath. U. L. Rev. 663

11. Zhangjin. Research on Private Copying in Copyright Law: From Printing Press to Internet [M]. Beijing: China University of Political Science and Law Press, 2009
12. Agostino G A. Healing Fair Dealing? A Comparative Copyright Analysis of Canada's Fair Dealing to U. K. Fair Dealing and U. S. Fair Use [J]. McGill Law Journal, 2008
13. David Vaver, Copyright, vol. 2 (1998) at 522 [unpublished, archived at Osgoode Hall Law School Library]
14. Carys Jane Craig, Fair Dealing and the Purposes of Copyright Protection (LL. M. Thesis, Queen's University, 2000) [unpublished]
15. Laddie, Prescott, Victoria. The Modern Law of Copyright and Designs [M]. 3ed. London: Butterworths, 2000
16. Michael Gast. For the Public Interest: The Future of Canadian Copyright Law [M]. Li Jing, trans. Beijing: Intellectual Property Publishing House, 2008
17. Litman. Digital Copyright [M]. Amherst: Promehteus Books, 2001: 178
18. Song Haiyan. Discussing the fair use of Chinese Law from the practice of copyright law in various countries: the thinking caused by the google library plan [J]. China Copyright, 2011, 1
19. Julie E. Cohen, et al. Copyright Law in the Global Information Economy [M]. Beijing: CITIC press, 2003: 494
20. Shan Xiaoguang, Liu Xiaohai. Judgment of the German Federal Constitutional Court on the Constitutional Freedom of Art and the Reasonable Citation Relationship of Copyright Law [J]. Intellectual Property Research, 2004, 1
21. Yang Heyi. New Changes and Characteristics of Japanese Copyright Law [J]. Strait Law, 2010, 1
22. United Nations Conference on Trade and Development, Center for International Trade and Sustainable Development. TRIPS Agreement and Development: Readings [M]. Cambridge University Press, 2005: 172 (non-public publication)
23. Yin Yuanyuan. Three-step Test Method: Is It Necessary to Add It into the "Copyright Law" [J]. China Intellectual Property Journal, 66
24. John Hartley. Creative Industry Reader [M]. Cao Shule, BaoJiannv, Li Hui, Trans. Beijing: Tsinghua University Press, 2007: 14

Chapter 3
Legal Relationship of the Rights Limitation System

"Abstract objects are the 'things' that mediate property relations between individuals in the case of intellectual property. In the case of tangibles a person can deprive another by taking the thing. But the nature of abstract objects permits of their simultaneous use and so deprivation of the object through use cannot take place."[1] A copyright system established based on such abstract objects needs to clarify the legal relationships around this object. Because the construction of any legal system is based on the legal relationship established or protected there from. Only when legal relationships are established can the interests be distributed among all parties in the legal relationship. This section first analyzes the subject of rights, the object of rights and the application of rights in the legal system of copyright. After the legal relationship and content of copyright are determined and delimited, this section defines the problems that shall be discussed regarding the subject of rights and the object of rights in the system of fair use of copyright, and systematically analyzes the rights and interests relationship resulted from fair use, a legal system. Current laws and theories seldom analyze the legal relationship in fair use systematically. Especially in the legislation, this "most difficult to say" system is mostly established by enumerating the specific circumstances that fair use can be applied. On the basis of the legal relationship of the copyright system, this section further introduces the legal relationship in the system of fair use within the copyright limitation system so as to understand this system in principle.

3.1 Legal Relationship of the Copyright System

Civil legal relationship refers to the social relationship regulated by civil law norms. It is the kind of social relationship that is recognized and protected by civil law, that complies with civil law norms, and that involves the content of rights and obligations.

---

[1] De Hos [1].

© Intellectual Property Publishing House 2021
S. Liu, *Rights Limitation in Digital Age*,
https://doi.org/10.1007/978-981-16-4380-4_3

The copyright system is a form of civil legal relationship. It regulates the rights and obligations of the author or the right holder and the user for their control and use of the work.

3.1.1 Subject

The 13th-century Franciscan monk St. Bernard Ventura said that there were four ways to write a book: the first type is people who can copy other people's books without making any changes or adding anything to the book. This type of person can only be called "copywriters". The second type of person copy from someone else's book, and add something that is not his/her own. This type of person is called "editors". The third type is people whose work include a little bit of their content as comment and a large part of contents from others' works. This type of person is called a "commentators". The fourth type of people is those who create a large part of content and add a little bit of others' content as confirmation. This kind of person is "authors".[2]

Among the subjects of the copyright system, the author is the main copyright subject, and is the original and complete copyright subject.[3] Chinese copyright law provides that copyright owners including authors, other citizens, legal persons or other organizations determined in accordance with the law. The subject of copyright is produced according to law. "There are little dispute in theory over who is 'copyright owner', the subject of copyright. The copyright owner may be the author or someone else who has been assigned with this right from the author. Therefore, the copyright owner can be either a natural person or a legal person. This is generally recognized in all countries with copyright laws."[4]

First of all, as a subject in the copyright system, natural persons are the most original creators of works, because only natural persons can create works in fields of literature, art and science. Natural persons create through intellectual activities, and attach invisible spirits and ideas to their works. Objectively, natural persons are the only factual authors of literary, artistic and scientific works.[5]

Second, in social life, in addition to natural persons, other subjects may also become the subjects of copyright system recognized by law through a manner such as the exchange of interests. They are called the "statutory authors".[6] Article 11 of the Brazilian Copyright Law stipulates that: the author of a literary, artistic or scientific work is a natural person who creates a work; for the circumstances provided in this Law, legal persons may also enjoy the protection obtained by the author. Article 49.1 further stipulates that when the author's right is transferred as a whole, the author's

---

[2] Manguel [2].

[3] Feng [3], p. 37.

[4] Zheng [4].

[5] Liu [5], p. 91.

[6] Liu [5], pp. 91–92.

3.1 Legal Relationship of the Copyright System 55

personal rights are still excluded from the transferable rights, indicating that the legal person is different from the natural person in status when being the copyright owner. Article 7 of the German Act on Copyright and Related Rights stipulates that the person who creates the work shall be deemed the author, and Article 2.2 emphasizes that personal intellectual creations alone shall constitute works within the meaning of this Law.

The UK Copyright Law has a more detailed definition on the identity of the author. Regarding the identity of the author, Article 9 stipulates that (1) In this part "author", in relation to a work, means the person who creates it. (2) That person shall be taken to be (aa) in the case of a sound recording, the producer; (ab) in the case of a film, the producer and the principal director; (b) in the case of a broadcast, the person making the broadcast or, in the case of a broadcast which relays another broadcast by reception and immediate re-transmission, the person making that other broadcast; (d) in the case of the typographical arrangement of a published edition, the publisher. (3) In the case of a literary, dramatic, musical or artistic work which is computer-generated, the author shall be taken to be the person by whom the arrangements necessary for the creation of the work are undertaken.

The U.S. Copyright Act explicitly stipulates the several circumstances of ownership of the copyright when discussing the content of copyrighted work and the copyright ownership. However, it does not directly define or categorize the copyright subject. Specifically, Article 201 stipulates the ownership of copyright: (a) Initial Ownership—Copyright in a work protected under this title vests initially in the author or authors of the work. The authors of a joint work are coowners of copyright in the work. (b) Works Made for Hire—In the case of a work made for hire, the employer or other person for whom the work was prepared is considered the author for purposes of this title, and, unless the parties have expressly agreed otherwise in a written instrument signed by them, owns all of the rights comprised in the copyright. (c) Contributions to Collective Works—Copyright in each separate contribution to a collective work is distinct from copyright in the collective work as a whole, and vests initially in the author of the contribution. The U.S. Copyright Act stipulates that the author of a work is the rights holder, but does not further distinguish whether the rights holder is a natural person and a legal person. Any rights holder may enjoy all copyright benefits provided in this Law.

3.1.2 Object

The object in a legal relationship means the object pointed to by the rights and obligations in a legal relationship. The applications in a legal relationship mainly include things, payment behaviors, intellectual creations and personality interests. Legal object is the legal form of certain interests. The purpose of establishing a legal relationship is to protect, acquire, and control this interest. The object of legal relationship is the intermediary to help realize the rights-obligations relationship. Therefore, the object of legal relationship is the benefit realized by the application pointed to by the legal relationship. This benefit is not the object itself, so the object of the legal relationship is interests rather than the application.

The academic community has different understandings of the concept of the object of copyright. First of all, the concept of the object of copyright is equated with the concept of application, opining that "the object and application of intellectual property fall within the same category".[7] Some say that "the object of copyright refers to the application that both the rights and obligations in the legal relationship of copyright are directed to. It is the creative intellectual creations embodied in a concrete form of certain objective existence, namely, literary, artistic, and scientific works."[8] Professor Zheng Chengsi believes that the object of copyright refers to a specific work.

The view that equates the object of copyright with application is derived from some civil law theories. In some civil law works, the object, target, and application of rights are often used interchangeably.[9] Wu Handong advocates the generalization of the object of intellectual property as a "knowledge product", with the object of copyright further divided into literary works, artistic works and scientific works. He believes that the objects of intellectual property are original creations that appear in different forms and occur in the fields of literature and art.[10] Professor Liu Chuntian believes that the object and application of intellectual property are two different things. The application of intellectual property is "knowledge" itself, and the object of intellectual property refers to the behavior that is targeted at the application and that can produce certain interest relationship.[11]

In the realm of real rights, transactions mean both the exchange of property and the exchange of property rights. Property rights cannot be discussed without control over the object. The property rights and the property indicated by the rights cannot be separated. Due to the uniqueness of object, the transaction of an object is the transaction of related rights. However, there is no object in the transaction of intellectual property, and the rights can be continuously copied on a new carrier without affecting the value of the matter. It is inversely proportional to the economic scarcity of natural objects. Therefore, within the framework of the legal relationship of intellectual property rights, rights are traded, and profits can be obtained by the trading of rights. Objects in legal relationship are behaviors achieved through various rights rather than the applications being traded.

3.1.3 Applications

(1)   Definition of works

---

[7] Wu [6], p. 36.

[8] Feng [3], p. 43.

[9] Wu [6], p. 36. See Jin [7].

[10] Wu [6], p. 40.

[11] Liu [5], pp. 8–9.

3.1 Legal Relationship of the Copyright System

In the Berne Convention, the concept of a work is expressed as: "[t]he expression 'literary and artistic works' shall include every production in the literary, scientific and artistic domain, whatever may be the mode or form of its expression."[12] Article 2 of the Regulations for the Implementing of the Copyright Law of China issued on 2002 describes the works in the Copyright Law as follows: "The term 'works' used in this Law shall mean original intellectual creations in the literary, artistic and scientific domain, insofar as they are capable of being reproduced in a certain tangible form."

The basic elements required for a copyrighted work are: (1) the work should be original; (2) the expression form of the work should be either literary, artistic, and scientific works. "The completion of a work should be the result of the author's own choice, selection, arrangement, design, and comprehensive description."[13]

Past experience shows that the application of the "idea-expression dichotomy" on the object of copyright protection is difficult in judicial practice.[14] While emphasizing the basic theory of protecting the form, the judges have to examine whether the works that involve similar "ideas" are substantial the same. Dr. Lu Haijun puts forward the concept of "substance of an expression" and "form of an expression" in his book "The Object of Copyright". He believes that there is a distinction between "substance of an expression" and "form of an expression" in the process of creation. At the same time, the inherent elements of a work determine that the "substance of an expression" exists independent of the "form of an expression". This pair of concepts further extended the "dichotomy of the ideological expression". First of all, the "substance of an expression" is the objective form of an expression rather than the idea itself, so it is not in the brain of the creator and is not illusory and unpredictable; second, the purpose to distinguish "substance of an expression" and "form of an expression" is to prove that there is an "substantial expression" behind a "symbolic expression."[15] "The perception of the existence of real foreign objects is not only the source of all knowledge materials, but also the basis of self-awareness and awareness of the internal state of the self."[16] The sensible appearance, as long as it is in direct contact with the object, is considered as being intuitive. Intellectuality does not directly contact the object, and the relationship between knowledge and object is indirect. The representation of intellectuality is not special, specific, but abstract, general, and can be applied to all applications of the same class. This is called a concept. Intellectuality forms concept, which is used to judge the application of thinking.[17] Post-Marxist cultural study defines culture as the process of production, circulation, and consumption of meanings.[18] The trick is to equate the production and function of knowledge with the production in Marx's economic theory. This

---

[12] Article 2.1, Berne Convention.

[13] Liu [5], p. 52.

[14] Tushnet [8].

[15] Lu [9].

[16] Qi [10].

[17] Russell [11], p. 50.

[18] Staller [12].

"product" is not necessarily a creation. Whether it is creation or reproduction, in the transaction process, there is no essential difference between knowledge products and the objects in traditional market trading. The development of culture has changed in the process of production and dissemination of knowledge, and impacts people's production methods, lifestyles, consumption patterns, etc. These impacts are determined by the symbolism brought about by the culture in circulation. "The significance of symbolism lies in that, people can convey the experience, the concept or the belief through the symbolism of the work, and finally achieve the purpose of mutual communication. The symbolic form is produced, constructed or used by a subject, who, when using these forms, is pursuing certain goals and trying to express their ideas or thoughts. The subject that creates and transfers the symbolic meaning communicate with the recipient based on a series of rules, experiences, and cultural influences. Due to individual differences, it is actually impossible for creators and audience to achieve complete agreement on the understanding of the object. The symbolic form is always influenced by the specific social and historical background. From each stage of its birth, output to acceptance, different subjects may have different interpretations."[19] The ideas embodied in knowledge can only be realized in practice, with its value achieved in exchange. "In the transmission of a work, that is, a symbolic form, the meaning it conveys and re-constructs in the process of acceptance may serve to support and replicate the background of production and acceptance. The meaning of the accepted and understood symbolic form may serve in various ways to maintain the structural social relations that are uniquely produced in the symbolic form or the background."[20] The artistic creation is not about its image, but also the idea involved. The two are interdependent and interchangeable. When an artist discovers a specific image, he/she would also feel the ideological power of the image; likewise, when he/she keenly captures the flash of a certain idea, he will then fully display the image.[21]

"Knowledge" must be associated with certain applications. Take a concept as an example, if it is not intuitively associated with certain experience, it is still an idea. Since there is no application, it is not knowledge.[22] Therefore, knowledge must be used to express an application and convey the meaning of the application. The process of acquiring knowledge is a process of understanding the application pointed to by knowledge. Therefore, "rather than a series of things—fictions, paintings, TV programs, or comedy, culture is a process, a series of practices. The focus in culture is on the production and exchange of meaning, which is the process of giving and acquiring meaning."[23] The definition of a protected work is not limited to the protection of the form, but also the meaning to be conveyed by the work. This is an important factor in evaluating "plagiarism". Such kind of plagiarism directly affects

---

[19] Thompson [13].

[20] See Footnote 19.

[21] Yin [14].

[22] Russell [11], pp. 63–64.

[23] Stuart [15], quoted from Staller [12].

3.1 Legal Relationship of the Copyright System

the rights of the original author. Thus, it is often not comprehensive to take "form" alone as the application of rights protection.

(2)   Types of works protected by copyright

The general provisions of the US Copyright Act on the object of copyright protection are: copyright protection subsists, in accordance with this title, in original works of authorship fixed in any tangible medium of expression, now known or later developed, from which they can be perceived, reproduced, or otherwise communicated, either directly or with the aid of a machine or device. Works of authorship include the following categories: (1) literary works; (2) musical works, including any accompanying works; (3) dramatic works, including any accompanying music; pantomimes and choreographic works; (4) pictorial, graphic, and sculptural works; (5) motion pictures and other audiovisual works; (6) sound recordings; and architectural works. In no case does copyright protection for an original work of authorship extend to any idea, procedure, process, system, method of operation, concept, principle, or discovery, regardless of the form in which it is described, explained, illustrated, or embodied in such work.

The Copyright Law of China clarifies the types of protected works, and in the Implementation Regulations of the Copyright Law, the list of protected works is more detailed, including: (1) written works are works expressed in written form, such as novels, poems, essays and thesis, etc. (2) oral works are works which are created in spoken words such as impromptu speeches, lectures and court debates, etc. (3) music works are such works as symphonic works and songs, with or without accompanying words, which can be sung or performed; (4) dramatic works are such works as dramas, operas and local art forms which are used for stage performance; (5) "quyi" works include such works as "xiangsheng" (cross talk), "kuaishu" (clapper talk), "dagu" (ballad singing with drum accompaniment) and "pingshu" (story-telling based on classic novels), which are all used mainly for being performed in a way involving recitation, singing, or both; (6) choreographic works are works which are or can be expressed in successive body movements, gestures and facial movements; (7) acrobatic art works are such works as acrobatics, magic and circus which can be expressed in body movements and in technique way; (8) works of fine art are two-or three-dimensional works created in lines, colors or other medium which, when being viewed, impart aesthetic effect, such as paintings, works of calligraphy, sculptures and works of architecture; (9) architectural works are works which are works in architectural building or expressed in similar format, when being viewed, impart aesthetic effect; (10) photographic works are the kind of artistic works created by recording images of objective matters on light-sensitive materials or other media with the aid of devices; (11) cinematographic works and works which are created in analogous shooting cinematographic works are works shot on certain media and consisting of a series of related images which are played with the aid of suitable devices or transferred in other ways, together with accompanying sounds or not; (12) pictorial works are such works as drawings of engineering designs and product designs which are designed for the purpose of actual construction and manufacturing, and maps, sketches and other graphic works showing geographic phenomena and demonstrating the fundamentals or the structure of a thing; (13) model works are three-dimensional works which are drawn to certain scale according to format and structure of a thing for the purpose of exhibition, testing and viewing.

3.1.4 Relationship Between Rights and Obligations

The legal relationship of copyright is the relationship between rights and obligations in the copyright system. In this relationship, the rights subject implements a specific behavior (ie, the object of copyright), on the application of copyright, that is, the work… thereby generating the relationship between specific rights and obligations corresponding to the specific behavior. In implementing an act of obtaining rights or fulfilling obligations, the copyright system adjusts the legal system which takes the act of creating and changing the relationship between rights and obligations as the object. The fact that works exist objectively does not change any legal relationship, or generate any interests. Only by a series of acts such as copying, distributing, and performing, will the interests related to the book be generated. Therefore, the status of a "Christmas Hymn" in the copyright is the same as the status of a laptop in real right. They are the application of rights and the application pointed to by the rights. Only with the behavior or status of possession or use of this laptop can the property rights of the right holders be realized. For example, only with the behavior of publishing and distributing a novel by Dickens can the moral and material interests of Dickens be realized.

3.2 Legal Relationship of the Fair Use System

3.2.1 Subject

The subject in the fair use system refers to all the persons who use the works. They are the users of the works as opposed to the copyright holders. People who are qualified users must obtain the copyrighted works through legal means. In the system of copyright limitation, the law gives the user implement the right of the copyright owner. The part of the rights sacrificed by the copyright owner is for the unspecified public.

3.2.2 Object

The use here should refer to the use of the substantive content expressed in the work. Depending on the specific purpose of use, the object of fair use can be divided into privately copied works for repeated self-entertainment and works to be used for re-creation.

1. Private copying behavior for personal use. As discussed in this Chapter, it is necessary to clarify that private copying in the fair use system is a purely copying act that is different from the use of copyrighted works for re-creation. The object of private copying is a complete copyrighted work (such as the reproduction of music). The purpose of this copying behavior is only for users to reuse the work itself at another time and place. Therefore, the object in the private copying act is the same as the object of copyright.

2. Personal use behavior for innovation. In some specific cases, the law allows users to reproduce to a certain degree protected works primarily for reasons of comment, education, or for news reporting. Recent legislative trends in different countries indicate that such purpose of use no longer applies to the fair use system. They now tend to adjust the relationship between the user and the right holder through the statutory licensing system. Statutory license requires a relatively mature copyright collective management mechanism to serve as a powerful guarantee to protect the author's rights and interests. The copyright collective management system is an intensive way of exercising and protecting rights and an important way to solve the licensing problem of direct dissemination of works.

3.2.3 Application

The application in fair use and the application in copyright should be the same. However, in the fair use, as there are different purposes of use, the subject in fair use, the user, will also be different depending on different use behavior when they control the application. First of all, for the purpose of personal use, including the complete or incomplete reproduction and study of the work, the value of the work may be reflected by all the whole works, such as when listening to musical works, and may be reflected by the value of a part of the work, such as using the work for private study. When a work is used for classroom teaching, the essence extracted from a masterpiece is enough to reflect the value of this book. At this time, the content or thought in the book becomes the user's materials to help express his ideas. Thus, the user uses the work within a range of less than or equal to the original work. Therefore, the applications in the fair use system are included in the copyright object, and are divided into complete or partial presentation. The user pays attention to the symbolic content.

3.2.4 Relationship Between Rights and Obligations

The subject of fair use is the counterpart of the copyright owner and the subject of the obligation of the copyright. The legal relationship of fair use is the right and obligation relationship within the framework of the copyright system resulted from non-copyright owners obtaining works through legal means, from the use of works, or from use of works by way of legally copying and using the intellectual content in the works. In this system, the user of a work is the subject of "right", and the right holder of the work is the counterpart. In civil legal relationships, in most cases, both parties enjoy rights and undertake obligations. In the copyright system, the right holder of a work is the subject enjoying the author's moral rights and property rights. In the transaction of a work, the user pays a consideration to the right holder to use the work, and the right holder has the obligation to enable the use his/her work by the buyer. This is similar to that rights and obligation relationships in the transfer of property rights. Apart from the rights and obligations relationship established in the system, this author believes that as an assumed right, the copyright owner monopolizes knowledge; and to protect knowledge as a kind of property, the rights of copyright owners need to be limited. In order to prevent abuse of rights, limitations and exceptions to copyright owner's rights are set in the copyright system, which is an obligation of the right holder and a right granted to the user. Therefore, regarding the legal relationship in fair use, we take the perspective of users of copyrighted works and discuss the subject, object and content in the legal relationship of the fair use system.

References

1. Peter De Hos. Intellectual Property Law Philosophy [M]. Zhou Lin, trans. Beijing: The Commercial Press, 2008: 32–33
2. Alvito Manguel. Reading History [M]. Wu Changjie, trans. Beijing: The Commercial Press, 2002: 72
3. Feng Xiaoqing. Copyright Law [M]. Beijing: Law Press, 2010
4. Zheng Chengsi. Copyright Law (I) [M]. Beijing: China Renmin University Press, 2009: 29
5. Liu Chuntian. Intellectual Property Laws [M]. 4th ed. Beijing: China Renmin University Press, 2009
6. Wu Handong. Research on Basic Issues of Intellectual Property [M]. 2nd ed. Beijing: China Renmin University Press, 2009
7. Jin Baolandeng. Comparative Study of Civil Legal System [M]. Beijing: Chinese People's Public Security University Press, 2001: 64
8. Tushnet R. Copy This Essay: How Fair Use Doctrine Harms Free Speech and How Copying Serves It [J]. Yale L. J., 2004, 114: 535, 544, 549, 550
9. Lu Haijun. Copyright Object Theory [M]. Beijing: Intellectual Property Publishing House, 2011: 117–120
10. Qi Liangji. Kant's Knowledge [M]. Beijing: The Commercial Press, 2000: 39
11. Russell. Human Knowledge: Its Scope and Limits [M]. Zhang Jinyan, trans. Beijing: The Commercial Press, 1983

References

12. John Staller. Introduction to Cultural Theory and Popular Culture [M]. 5 ed. Chang Jiang, trans. Beijing: Beijing University Press, 2010: 106
13. Thompson. Ideology and Modern Culture [M]. Gao Xian, trans. Nanjing: Yilin Press, 2005:181
14. Yin Guoming. Art Form is Not Just a Form [M]. Hangzhou: Zhejiang Literature and Art Publishing House, 1988:2
15. Hall Stuart (1997): "Introduction", in Representation, edited by Stuart Hall, London

Chapter 4
Types of Rights Limitation in Digital Technology Environment

"In the past 30 years, the development of Internet technology has intuitively demonstrated a hummingbird effect. The sharing of information has grown by orders of magnitude, pushing the original benefit distribution system to a chaotic state, easily surpassing the boundaries of knowledge and society", which makes the reform of the system imminent.

Within the framework of the copyright system, some "private copying" behaviors are list among the circumstance that fair use can be applied in the laws of most countries. However, objectively, due to the development of copying technology, the prohibiting of any form of or the allowing a part of "private copying" can neither fully protect right holders, nor guarantee the public interests. Therefore, it is necessary to make a distinction between the specific behaviors and purposes of use in private copying in practice. First of all, we should distinguish between copying behavior for the purpose of personal learning and entertainment and copying behavior for the purpose of innovation based on whether the copying behavior ultimately forms a new work. Secondly, it is necessary to make a distinction between statutory license and fair use based on the impact of innovation on the original rights holder.

© Intellectual Property Publishing House 2021
S. Liu, *Rights Limitation in Digital Age*,
https://doi.org/10.1007/978-981-16-4380-4_4

Another premise to be emphasized is that consumers need to obtain protected works through legal means. Consumers may either pay corresponding considerations for special works, or may use them for free with the right holders having granted the disseminator the privilege of free disseminating. Other means of obtaining a protected work are illegal, as they violate the interests of the right holders.

4.1 Private Copying

In modern copyright laws, there is no clear and satisfactory definition on private copying. Professor Julie Cohen once said that private copying has long been a "dirty little secret of the copyright system".[1] This reveals that the use behavior in real-life and the existing copyright cases are vastly different in quantity. In recent years, with the rapid spread of the private copying technology, this problem has become one of the most difficult puzzles to solve.

4.1.1 Classification of Private Copying

In most of theories that discuss private copying, there are different interpretations for the purpose of private copying. Personal use refers to the use of copyrighted works by various means for personal purposes, and copying is only one of them. The premise of the definition of private copying is the case of private copying permitted by law in fair use, and such copying itself is beyond the control of the right holder.

Private copying under the fair use system and private copying under the statutory licensing system should be distinguished. This distinction is based on whether the right holders should be paid corresponding remuneration for the copying. The "copying" here means that the user has exercised the right of copying that is a right of the rights holder. We need to distinguish whether such copying is free copying allowed by law, or the right holder need to be paid accordingly.

---

[1] Cohen [1].

4.1.2 Definition of Private Copying

4.1.2.1 Definition of Private Copying in the Traditional Copyright Framework

In the copyright limitation system, the consequences of private copying are divided into free copying in a fair use system and private copying under statutory license that requires payment of compensation.

Private copying is one of the ways by which individuals use protected works. This author believes that this concept should be interpreted both in a broad sense and a narrow sense. First of all, in the system of copyright, the provisions on the right of reproduction have both a broad and narrow sense. "The right of reproduction in a narrow sense is the right of reproduction in a strict sense. It generally only refers to a right to make a finished product in the same form, for example, copying a written work to generate books, magazines, newspaper, and the like. It also includes copying on a carrier different from an original carrier or copying by using different technologies."[2] Professor Zheng Chengsi considers that the right of reproduction can be understood from the broadest sense as all the rights to "reproducing" "the basic constitution" of the original work, including the right of publication. It changes the carrier or form of expression of the original work through translation, adaptation, broadcasting, recording, etc.[3] Article 10.5 of China's Copyright Law provides that the right of reproduction, namely, the right to produce one or more copies of the work by means of printing, xeroxing, rubbing, sound recording, video recording, duplicating, or re-shooting, etc. This is a narrow interpretation of the right of reproduction. When discussing the issue of private copying, it is necessary to define the boundaries of this copying behavior to make it consistent with the concept of the right of reproduction in the copyright system. In addition, the term "personal use" is used in place of the broad sense private copying, which refers to other forms of use of non-pure copying of protected works.

The Berne Convention and some copyright writings define private copying in the fair use system as copying behaviors by non-right holders. Such behavior usually meets the following conditions: the subject of the copying behavior is a non-right holder, namely, the user; the copying behavior is for the purpose of personal use; the number of copies is small; the nature of copying is non-profit; and the copying shall not compromise the interests of the right holder of the work. Professor Zhang Jin summarized the private copying behavior as a small number of repeated reproductions of copyrighted works for personal use.[4] In Article 171.2 of the Copyright Section of the Egyptian Intellectual Property Protection Law, the number of copies of the work for personal use is limited to one copy; the use of the copy shall not conflict with the normal use of the work, nor shall it unreasonably damage the legitimate rights of the

---

[2] Liu [2].

[3] Zheng [3].

[4] Zhang [4].

author or the copyright holder. This is a more explicit limitation on the number of copies of private copying behavior.

4.1.2.2 Private Copying in the Fair Use System in the Digital Environment

From the traditional definition, we can conclude that the elements of private copying are as follows: the purpose is for personal use; copies same as the original are produced objectively; and the use of the copy shall not cause substantial damage to the rights holder. However, it should be noted that the producing of copies, a very important point in the above elements, is based on the traditional copyright law, with the premise of the objective existence of things. For example, the behavior of copying certain pages of a book in a library requires a carrier, namely papers, for the copying. However, under the condition of digital technology, people no longer need to "copy" an original to achieve private copying. In the Internet environment, reproduction of works does not require the copying of the original, and this brings challenges to the traditional definition of private copying. Therefore, under the condition of digital technology, the right holder pays more attention to the number of times that his works are "uses" than the number of times that his works are "copied". Therefore, it is necessary to redefine private copying.

In the context of digital technology, private copying that is fair use refers to the way of reproducing a work through various means for the purpose of personal use, with the premise of not causing substantial damage to the rights holder. The element of the purpose of personal use will not be further illustrated. Regarding the element "shall not cause substantial damage to the rights holder", this author believes that this element should mean that when a user first obtains the protected work, he should obtain it through legal means. Taking academic articles acquisition on the Internet as an example, users can obtain free articles from public resources, or they can get articles by means of paying remuneration, which mainly depends on how the rights holder provides protected works to the public.

4.1.3 The Significance of Imposing Strict Limitations on of Private Copying Behavior in Fair Use

Under the traditional fair use system, the behavior itself is difficult to be categorized, but can only be investigated on a case by case basis. The criteria used in the investigation are not static. Therefore, there should be a strict distinction between the private copying behavior that is fair use and the behavior for innovation. The traditional infringement standard for private copying is the number of copies. Each copy of the original works is complete and unmodified, and there is no change in the way the copies are used. For example, people often convert songs from CDs to

MP3 at home, so that they can be uploaded to personal network space for off-site enjoyment without having to go out with the CD. In this way, as long as people go to a place with Internet, they can play the music they want to listen to with the corresponding equipment. This kind of copying is copying in the strict sense, as it does not change the way the works is used, namely, listing to music. Another example is, some users on social networks retake childhood photos through digital cameras and put them on the Internet to share with others. By doing so, the way of appreciating the same photographic work has not changed. Innovation involves not only the number of copies of a work, but ultimately the creation of new works. In other words, the distinction between private copying and innovative use should be based on whether a new work is produced. The final result of such copying of innovative nature has destroyed the integrity of the original work. The concept of innovation is stressed here, that is, people do not enjoy a work in a way designed by the author of the original work, but might change the original way of enjoying a work based on the user's ideas. For this purpose, the original work becomes the material for innovation by the users who care more about the relationship between the factors available in the original work and what they want to create, and focus more on how the original work can be used by him. The result of such copying has objectively impacted the original rights holder to a certain extent, which may either be positive or negative impact.

4.1.4 Compensation System

Important international conventions on copyright include the Berne Convention for the Protection of Literary and Artistic Works, the WIPO Copyright Treaty, the WIPO Performances and Phonograms Treaty, and the copyright laws of some large countries, including the U.S. Copyright Act of 1976, the Italian Copyright Law of 1981, the Canadian Copyright Act before the entry into force of the C-32 Act in October 1999, the current Australian Copyright Act, etc. None of these laws clearly stipulates the legality of "private use", let alone the design of a system that imposes a "private copying tax" on manufacturers and sellers of reproduction devices and media, although these laws can deduct different conclusions on protecting "the right of reproduction" in the field of "private use" or protecting the "right of production" of the users through the "fair use doctrine".

The premise of the copyright compensation system is private copying. The compensation system is in fact not involved in fair use. Professor Zhang Jin believes that the main reason that the compensation system, with the nature of a correction to fair use, is not equal to the statutory licensing system, is that the nature of compensation is compensation due to fair use behavior, and cannot be equivalent to right consideration.[5] In addition, what the rights holders are most worried about is that if they think that the payment of compensation is regarded as obtaining authorization,

---

[5] See Footnote 4.

the scope of rights of the rights holder will be narrowed and the copyright owner will lose the equal negotiation status in the license agreement.

Since the 1950s, the German Society for Musical Performance and Mechanical Reproduction Rights (GEMA) has filed infringement warnings and lawsuits against manufacturers and sellers of recording equipment. The video recorders, photocopiers, and audio recorders that were invented in the 1970s enabled millions of American consumers to reproduce protected works and opened up the era of private and cheap use. New types of devices that have spread rapidly in the past decade or so have been accepted by the public in a more rapid and widespread manner and these devices are considered "legitimate". The number of protected works obtained through private copying is far greater than that legally obtained through authorization, and the number of such unauthorized uses is staggering.[6] However, the compensation system is a solution for problems brought about by technological development.

The compensation system actually detaches some of the private copying for the purpose of personal appreciation from the "fair use" system, so such private copying should be detached both institutionally and theoretically.[7] The compensation for the rights holder is mainly realized by the levying of "private copying tax".[8] Strictly speaking, the law should classify this part of reproduction as a kind of "statutory license".

4.1.5 Private Copying for Musical Works

The traditional model of music industry is not compatible with the way people consume music in the Internet environment. The music industry has begun to use technology to find new business models that can solve this problem so that it would be easier for consumers to access music. At the same time, the protection on content needs to be taken as seriously as before to ensure the benefits of musicians. The most important factors affecting the purchase of music online are the popularity of portable players and the support of broadband. Digital music players have replaced tapes, CDs, and Walkmans that were popular in the twentieth century. In 2006, the sales volume of portable music players was about 120 million units. By 2011, in addition to the single-function portable player, more people downloaded music by using iPhone and mobile device with an android system.

In the past 30 years, music videos have been broadcast to the public through one-way media (such as television and public radio stations). On this single platform, music videos have to be shared in the market with television programs of various forms such as news programs and entertainment programs. However, in just a few

---

[6] Lohmannfy [5].

[7] Feng and Wei [6].

[8] For example, the compensation system for "Audio and Video Reproduction at Home" behavior in the United States of America-Audio Home Recording Act of 1992.

4.1 Private Copying

years, music videos can be spread independently through an interactive communication platform, the Internet. This transformation is vast, but the growth of the sharing of illegal musical works has been the main reason for the declining sales of legal music over the past decade. Law should ensure that the rights holder enjoys the copyright of works reproduced from the original work. However, thousands of users of digital music players are acting against this system. Unless technical measures to prevent copying can be found, such behavior can only be legally pardoned through a fair use system. With the positive policies adopted by laws of different countries to protect the copyright of digital works, the percentage of the sales of digital music in total music sales raise from 5% in 2005 to 20% in 2008. In 2010, about 29% of industry revenue came from digital music, totaling $4.9 billion. Music downloads remain the main source of digital music revenue.[9]

The development of Internet technology no longer require the owning of a music in order to enjoy the music. This objective phenomenon actually makes the "first sale doctrine" of copyright no longer applicable to enjoying music online. Although the Digital Music Report of the International Federation of the Phonographic Industry (IFPI) shows that music downloads are still the main source of digital music revenue, the new network technology will also have a further impact on people's choice, namely, the cloud technology may impact the law. Compared with the traditional way of accessing music, the following features are available for accessing music through the Internet. Firstly, users can directly find the music they want through tools such as search engines. The traditional method is limited by time and space, as the users who want to find a music disc need to visit the disc sales store during business hours, and would often be disappointed. Because physical stores are affected by factors such as area, supply, and copyright imports, it is difficult for users to find the most popular music CDs abroad. Secondly, users can have a variety of choices, for example, in the way of obtaining music, they can choose to download for free or to pay for download. In addition, they can put their favorite songs in playlists on the network space without having to download music to their own hard drive. Thus, they can enjoy their favorite music anytime, anywhere with the support of Internet hardware devices. Thirdly, users can choose different singles from different singers without having to buy the entire disc. Fourthly, users can listen to a clip of a song before deciding on a purchase.

Internet music providers usually offer paid-for or free music download services to the public. In 2009, the monthly visits of YouTube by global users reached 450 million (Chinese users might be excluded from this data due to restrictions on Internet access). It is worth pondering that the entire intellectual property system no longer relies on monopoly status to obtain benefits. When a novelist provides one of her novels to the public free of charge, she finds that her income from royalties are actually growing, because more people are willing to see more of this author's works and are willing to pay considerations for more works after reading her work that is provided free of charge. Record companies have also discovered that offering

---

[9] IFPI. Digital Music Report (2006–2010).

free concerts on the Internet boosts their record sales; more and more independent creators find their audience and profited from them.[10]

A more rigorous copyright protection environment makes rights holders choose to voluntarily renounce their rights in the Internet economy environment that were previously regarded as treasures, in exchange for commercial interests and economic returns in a broader sense. This could not have been achieved by the fair use system. However, a tolerant attitude towards the fair use system may cause large losses to right holders, as it is difficult for users to develop new services and business models to share benefits through cooperation with right holders.

Music is a special form in private copying. Music is different from movies. People record TV programs and enjoy them at another time or place. They may also enjoy them multiple times, but mostly no more than 10 times. Even if people copy the purchased movie DVD to a computer or other media and invite friends to enjoy it together, the times of this copying behavior is also extremely limited. However, people will never "take it easy" for their favorite music. They will enjoy it at home, while driving, and at work, and even use them as ringtones of their phones. People may listen to the same song dozens of times. Music as a form of work has the vitality and temptation to be continuously consumed, and is an art form that can be used and expressed most easily. When the entertainment industry strongly advocates extending the term of copyright protection, and the applicable situation of fair use is increasingly restricted, the record industry becomes increasingly depressed. This embarrassing situation in the protection of musical works has been disappointing to music creators. For example, most Chinese pop musicians have given up writing for singers in a traditional way, and are more enthusiastic about music creations for film and television works that can guarantee relatively high returns. After several years of downturn, more independent musicians were born in a way of profiting that is different from that of the traditional record industry. Many music writers put their works on the Internet for paid-for or free download by the public. They work independently, and no longer rely on record companies to make their music into songs, advertise for the songs, and spread them through traditional media. The wail of record companies today is much like those of the unemployed artisans in the early days of the industrial revolution. With technical support, recording equipment is becoming more popular and cheaper. Singers with high requirements on the recording environment may choose a professional recording studio to complete their works. Nowadays, the more popular way is to use a computer, software and a microphone to inputs sound into the computer and complete a song. After the creation of the works, many creators put them on the Internet for people to use for free, and those good works will be rewarded. But this reward is no longer limited by the traditional system.

---

[10] Fisher [7].

4.2 Copying for Innovation Purpose

The concept of intellectual property, the idea that certain ideas can be owned by others, was born with the Enlightenment in Europe. Only when people begin to believe that knowledge comes from the human mind that uses sensation, rather than by reading ancient articles and acquiring knowledge from Divine Enlightenment can people be regarded as the creators of new ideas and, thus, become a communicator for all other people's ideas and not just as a communicator of eternal truth.[11]

4.2.1 Copying for Innovation Purpose

4.2.1.1 Scope of Innovation

In this section, private copying and innovation-oriented copying in fair use are distinguished according to the purpose of copying behavior. Innovation-oriented copying behavior is directly associated with innovation, that is, this personal use behavior is a circumstance of fair use for the purpose of innovation. Whether it is direct quotation or deduction, full quotation or partial interception, the part that is used will become part of a new work, and will be used in a new expression to show the citer's thoughts.

4.2.1.2 Significance of Limiting the Scope of Innovative Use

Digital technology provides a solution to market failures, thus making the scope of fair use increasingly smaller. In addition to the need to reconstruct the copyright rights limitation system and impose stricter regulations on fair use, for the purpose of public interest and encouraging innovation, the institutional design on the nature and limitations on personal use behavior will affect the survival of the fair use system.

How to position personal use behavior for innovation purposes in the new technology environment is an important issue in considering the existence of fair use. The existence of the innovation-oriented fair use system will raise two questions. First, why should judicial solutions to fair use is based on private and orderly market solutions? If innovation is a blessing for the copyright industry under new technology, those peers should be willing to take the initiative to authorize their works to attract technology investment in a certain, free-to-use way. However, at a time when the market is imperfect, innovative is unlikely. Second, what if innovation is not a supplement to copyright, but instead destroys the enthusiasm of the innovators. The copyright law should respond to this to distinguish between the situation before- and after-creation, and to rebalance interests. Based on the fact that the impact of any particular innovation is difficult to predict in advance, perhaps an ex post fixation can

---

[11] Hesse [8].

build a better situation. In other words, instead of providing an innovative environment based on fair use, a statutory licensing model is better. Because under statutory license, users do not have to worry about authorization, and rights holders will share the benefits of innovative products with users.

In general, copyright law creates property interests, encourages creators, communicators, and the public in various markets to participate in transactions. This will lead to re-innovation and redistribution and enable more people to acquire knowledge in order to create more works with the same. However, imperfect market conditions may hinder the efficiency of the transactions, or because people do not protect the non-monetary value of the market. Some critics suggest that enforcement of copyright laws might jeopardize important privacy interests when too much interference with private copying is involved. Some others suggest that such law enforcement activities might violate the concept of personal property. For either consumers or copyright owners, cost control is essential in any transaction, therefore third-party intervention mechanism becomes necessary.

Two different innovations need to be identified. On the one hand, for the first innovation, it is necessary to meet the public's demand for knowledge acquisition, and to contribute to the education to promote the quality of the people. In terms of the system, the law should leave a fair use space for the use of academic research results, criticism and comments. On the other hand, for the achievements of innovation, the success of the second innovation is inseparable from the original right holder. The law should share the return of the latter with the original author. Based on the two different innovations, both purely fair use or infringement that is determined to be used without authorization is inappropriate.

4.2.2 Relationship Between Rational Use and Innovation

4.2.2.1 Innovation in Literary Works

In the sixteenth century, the increasing circulation of books, newspapers, and magazines influenced the views of writers on society. They reflected the spirit of readers of that era as writers. They left the study and created in the printing house. The role that the printing house played, i.e., bringing inspiration to the exchange of ideas, was like the role played by the US post office during the US information exchange explosion.[12] Therefore, those printing businessmen who first controlled the printing office and the cultural focus of the era published books in the name of authors. This may explain why originally "its true purpose is to protect the fiscal assets that accrue to the copier (publisher) of the work".[13] The Copyright Law is intended to give businessmen the legal sanction to copy works, usually for sale, belonging to someone,

---

[12] See Chandler and Cortada [9].

[13] Gantz and Rochester [10].

4.2 Copying for Innovation Purpose

i.e., the nominal creator or artist. The copyright law never was, nor ever will be the legal protection for the creator, at least not in a fiduciary way.[14]

Of the provisions on the fair use system of different countries, fair use mostly occurs when a new work has been produced, whether the use of the original work meets the conditions for fair use. In the process creating a literary work, the amount of content cited from another works is an important factor in determining whether the citing behavior is fair. In *Religious Technology Center v. Netcom On Line Communication services*, the court stated that although the law supports critical use, but if the "criticism" is just a copying of the majority of the plaintiff's work—sometimes even the whole of the work—with few comments at the best, the defense of fair use is obviously inappropriate.[15] When we talk about creativity and imagination, individuals shall be the starting point.[16] No one lives in a vacuum, even in a dream; our imagination is influenced by interactions with others, including direct contact with others, or through the influence of literature, art, movies, computer games, etc.[17]

In the twenty-first century, there are many organizations in Europe and the United States that fight for legitimating interests of piracy. They are also known as "piracy parties". These organizations view the copyright system as a stumbling block to transform commercial interests into cultural promotion. Throughout the nineteenth century, the dishonorable piracy system licensed by the United States has always been a pain in the hearts of British writers, although it is generally believed that this policy of the United States benefits the general public in the United States, and lets them receive good education in low-cost cultural environment. However, cultural historians may not be grateful for this system. Although it has been more than 200 years since the Mayflower landed on the continental United States, American writers are still waving the flag to get away from the impact of British literature. If the patent system of the United Stated is considered to have brought about a leap in industrialization in the United States, its negative copyright system might have inhibited the development of American literature and art.

4.2.2.2 Innovation in Film Works

In the Berne Convention, films become objects of copyright protection. However, among its member states, the form of protection for this type of work still differs greatly.

The birth of the moving pictures is the result of a series of inventions in the field of optics and photography. Originally it was showed as plots composed of continuously shot photos. In 1891, Edison applied for a camera patent for the "kinetograph" and applied for a viewing device patent for the "film viewing mirror". Edison did not personally participate in the promotion of this technology; he gave the rights to

---

[14] See Footnote 13.

[15] No.C-95020091 RMW, N. D. Cal. Field Sept. 22, 1995.

[16] Howkins [11, 12]. Quoted from Hartley [13].

[17] Hartley [13], p. 9.

others. In the following years, in the United States and several European countries, film screening studios appeared one after another. To get better viewing effect, this kind of studio could only accommodate one viewer.

Film was not initially accepted as a new form of art. It was only regarded by the public as a kind of entertainment or a new achievement during scientific progress. But this form of expression raises questions about copyright protection: the first is about protecting films from competitors and unlicensed cinema owners; the second is about whether movies violate the rights of other forms of work already available.[18]

Digital technology has a great impact on the way that traditional movies are filmed and produced. Films produced by new methods emerge, bringing unlimited impact and imagination to the audience, and challenges to the traditional legal system. Every aspect of the film industry is accompanied by major changes in digital technology. First of all, the filming of a movie is no longer the work of several cameras. In Hollywood studios, actors are mostly performing in the empty blue screen space, and the film images are finally completed through various stitching techniques. Even if people go to the cinema to enjoy movies, there are a variety of viewing options (they can choose traditional 2D screens or IMAX giant screen movies; they can wear glasses to enjoy 3D movies, or sit on a seat that can swing with the picture and enjoy the 4D movie in an immersive way). Movies are spread rapidly over the Internet because of digital compression technology. People can choose to go to the cinema to contribute to the box office, or they can buy a CD to watch at home. The most popular way today is to directly access video sites. People can watch movies at home, in the subway, in buses, in airport halls, etc., wherever they have Internet hardware support. People's lifestyle has changed. In addition to the changes in the film industry, the emergence and popularity of new audiovisual works also affects the application problem of existing laws.

In the book "Free Culture", the author tells us the status quo of the fair use system with a small story. A documentary producer learned of a documentary about opera actors. In a scene where the actors were resting in the backstage, the cartoon "The Simpsons" was playing on the TV in the background. This coincidence led the director to think that the state of the opera actors in the background was presented in an intriguing way. Due to the low-cost investment in the documentary, it was released after many years. The producer of the documentary believed that only 4.5 s of the footage is copyrighted and worked hard to obtain authorization. She contacted the cartoon producer, the film company, and its parent company Fox, hoping to get authorization. However, the whopping price offered by the rights holder made the producer finally give up using the 4.5 s animation. Although in the eyes of lawyers, this use behavior is fair use, most producers are reluctant to act rashly, although fair use means that there is no need to obtain a license or even no mandatory payment. In legal practice, the boundaries of this setting are still ambiguous and difficult to judge, but the consequences of crossing the border may be very serious.

---

[18] Kamina [14].

4.2 Copying for Innovation Purpose

Therefore, for many creators, there are very few circumstances of truly effective fair use. Although the law clarifies the purpose of this system, it fails to clearly specify the threshold of such application. Therefore, it is difficult to achieve the initial goals of fair use system design in practice. This rigid belief in the protection of rights has made the system go to an extreme. In the end, this documentary had to be "retouched" in a certain sense, which is against the spirit of documentary that aims to show people the facts in life.[19]

The multimedia works completed using digital technology, which are presented as audiovisual works, are very close to the way in which films are presented to people. How to deal with this types of works and whether to give such works the same protection that film works enjoy need to be further studied.

In the summer vacations of the last 10 years, there is a movie called "American Pie". The most distinctive feature is that it is a parody series of comedy movies. One of its most anticipated factors each year is how the director intends to let the characters in the show "spoof" the so-called classic plot in a series of popular movies of that year. The law allows this parody, not only because these episodes come together to form a new work, but also because what is reproduced in the new work is the "factor" in the original work, not a simple copying. In the following section, we are going to discuss the status of parody in fair use. The "innovation" in the self-media era is illustrated taking the "dancing baby case" as an example.

In February 2007, Stephanie Lenz posted a 29-s video on YouTube. In this video, her 13-month old baby was dancing with Prince's "Let's Go Crazy" playing in the background. Although the audio quality of the song that can be heard for about 20 s in this video is muffled, it was still requested to be deleted. In June 2007, Universal, the copyright owner of Let's Go Crazy, sent YouTube a DMCA takedown notice, claiming that the video infringed on Universal's copyright to the song. YouTube removed this video and notified Lenz of the deletion and allegations of infringement. At the end of June 2007, Lenz sent a counter-notice to YouTube, claiming that her use of the song clip constituted "fair use" and uploaded and forwarded the video again. After six weeks, the YouTube forwarded the video. In July 2007, Lenz filed a lawsuit against Universal who uses a DMCA notice in bad faith and asked the court to support her use of the copyrighted song.

After several years in this case, the 9th Circuit Court of Appeals issued its final judgment in September 2015. The court required that before issuing a notice of infringement, the rights holder should first consider whether the use of the infringing work constitutes fair use, that is, whether the premise of the use of material is "authorized by the right holder" or is based on "the provisions of the law". Otherwise the rights holder shall bear the legal liability of false statements. The positive significance of the judgment is that it restrains the abuse of the "notice-and-takedown" right of the rights holder. In the safe harbor principle for protecting "Online Service Providers", if the "notice-and-takedown" right is used without first evaluating fair use, this system will be tilted to the right holder instead of the Online Service Providers.

---

[19] Lessig [15].

4.2.3 Fair Use and Parody

4.2.3.1 Meaning of Parody

First of all, burlesque or parody is not a legal concept. In foreign cases on parody, the term "parody" is often used to discuss the issue of parody in fair use system. "Parody" has two meanings in the "Encyclopedia Britannica": one is the imitation of poetry; the other is the imitation of works, and to the creative reworking of musical works.[20] The parody and satire in the drama evolves from the imitation of poetry in poetics. Similarly, this form of expression is consistent with the theory that drama originates from poetry. "Centuries ago parody was a very real part of the system of literary review."[21]

In modern culture, parody realizes the reconstruction of the texts through imitation and transformation. It has a special purpose and reflects an intertextuality relationship.[22] In the parody work, the text, structure or plot of the original work is the code of the communication between the viewer and the parody work. Article 47 of the Brazilian Copyright Law has special provisions for parody, that is, "pastiches" and satirical imitation are not an actual reproduction of the original, nor do they cause damage in any way, and should be allowed.

Parody is an ancient form of artistic expression whose roots can be traced back to the ancient Greek period and it is also one of the expressions used by modern artists. It is undeniable for both writers and jurists that to evaluate a work by parody is irreplaceable. As a form of satirical work, a parody expression can easily explain the criticisms in culture. In politics, culture, social relations and other aspects, parody works can often become the mirror that reflects the epitome of real society. By creation, authors draw the attention of the public and make the original works the targets of their mockery. The Supreme Court of the United States has defined parody as making use of the characteristics of the original work to satire; as parody is based on the works of predecessors, to a certain extent it is necessary to copy and embezzle the prior works.[23] Only when the audience knows the prior works can the characteristics of parody works be reflected, otherwise the public can only recognize one single work, and will not have different resonances based on the same work.

If the author of a parody used the material of the prior work without the permission of the prior author, this may be a manifestation of infringement. Copyright grants authors special monopoly rights based on the work, and fair use excludes such unauthorized use when determining infringement. If the prior work is used to create a new work, and the substantial elements of the new work are different from the original

---

[20] Encyclopedia Britannica.

[21] Parody and the Law of Copyright [J/OL]. Fordhan Law Review, 1961, 29(3). http://ir.lawnet.for dham.edu/flr/vol29/iss3/7/.

[22] "Intertextuality" was proposed by Kristeva in Semiotics in 1969, meaning the relationship between discourse or text and other discourses or text. See also: Guo [16].

[23] Jonathan [17].

4.2 Copying for Innovation Purpose

work, this behavior might be defined as fair use, and parody in this case may be defined as fair use.

Taking the parody in music as an example, the historical image of music, as a symbol, plays the role of giving suggestions and metaphor in the work, thus attracting the attention of the audience to something they have experienced. Eventually, the original meaning of historical image was alienated by a special treatment, and then resulted in strange expressions. For one thing, it stimulates the listener's aesthetic passion, for another, it implies the unique meaning (satire, irony or reinforcement) expressed by the composer in a stark contrast, so that the exploration and perseverance in art reflected by the traditional deviation or rebellion by the composer can be elucidated by the symbolism.[24] The purpose of parody or the original intention of parody to change the work may determine whether a parody is a fair use, for example, to create a new work with an expression style unique to the original author, to satirize or tease the author's style. In this case, it does not actually involve material infringement of any work.

4.2.3.2 Cases Related to Parody

(1) Cases where parody is determined as infringing on the grounds of commercial interests

Regarding mimicry, the earliest case that involve an alleged infringement of mimicry is the *Bloom & Hamlin v. Nixon* case of 1903. The court ruled that a parody did not infringe on the original work, because the original work has been re-created. The key for this case is whether the mimicry is of "good faith",[25] if not, the singer will be prohibited from using the protected work in a "roundabout" manner.

Another early case related to parody was the *Hill v. Whalen & Martell, Inc* case.[26] The author of the cartoon work Mutt and Jeff created a popular cartoon piece. In a period of about three years, the royalties that author received from his copyright cartoon was $ 60,000 to 70,000. The defendant created two characters, Nutt and Giff, in his work In Cartoon land, with the images of these two characters similar to characters in the plaintiff's copyrighted works. The final judgment stated that although "a copyrighted work is subject to fair criticism, serious or humorous", in this case, the defendant's use behavior had an adverse market impact on the plaintiff, so it was not a fair use.

(2) Fair use for the purpose of "criticism and comment"

Any parody with the purposes of criticism and comment is fair use. This is based on the "freedom of speech" in the Constitution. In this regard, the most typical and influential case is *Campbell v. Acuff-Rose Music, Inc.*

---

[24] Ma [18].

[25] 125F.977(C.C.E.D.Pa.1903).

[26] 220Fed.359(S.D.N.Y.1914).

80   4 Types of Rights Limitation in Digital Technology Environment

The legal application of how parody works should be positioned in copyright is very complicated and uncertain. There is no standard and explicit statement on how to define which types of parody form or parody works are fair use. In the *Campbell v. Acuff-Rose Music, Inc.* case, we can see the discussion of the relationship between monopoly on copyright and the right to freedom of speech in the U.S. Copyright Act and the First Amendment to the U.S. Constitution.

In 1989, the 2 Live Crew, a rock band, made a rock version of Roy Orbison's ballad "Oh, Pretty Women" originally composed in 1969. The rock band's re-composition of this classical Caucasian's song was clearly intended to ridicule the Caucasian-centered rock trends that they thought were decadent and mediocre. In this case, many interested parties in the relevant industries expressed different views. For example, the rights holder of the musical works considered that any unauthorized adaptation for commercial use was unacceptable. However, many songwriters believe that if in the new work the purpose is to "reform the original work, in the process of innovating the work in accordance with the needs of society, a limited part of the original copyrighted work is used and transformed, then the parodist should be supported."[27]

Although in this case, the parody that constitutes fair use cannot be judged under the four factors of statutory fair use, it is clear that the court paid more attention to the important role of innovation behavior. If this ironic-oriented adaptation is denied, it will be a serious blow to most creations. Similarly, for the sake of public interest, the importance of "freedom of speech" in this case is prominent. In addition, the court also held that "satire can provide social benefit." Here, the court set its attention to the creator's advance preparation, when creating a new work in the process. The court held that parody, like other comment and criticism, may claim fair use under Copyright Act of 1976, 17 U. S. C. § 107. The court also held that 2 Live Crew's version "Oh, Pretty Women" thereafter departed markedly from the original for its own ends, and demonstrated its own characteristics. By altering the drum beat, interposing singers' distinctive sounds, and overlaying the music with solos in different keys, it brought the feeling of a new work.

The *Elsmere Music, Inc. v. National Broadcasting Co.* case[28] is a fair use case for the parody of public relations campaign in New York City. Saturday Night Live (SNL) used the song "I Love New York" and recomposed it to "I Love Sodom". United States Court of Appeals for the Second Circuit held that parodist's use of the tune of "I Love New York" was protected fair use. The extensive use might still be fair use, provided that the parody was built upon the original, used the original as a known element of modern culture and contributed something new for humorous effect or commentary. After reasoning, the Federal Circuit Court of Appeals for the Second Circuit affirmed that "the distinction between parody and satire is difficult to discern". The court needs to judge whether the use forms a new, effective satire or

---

[27] Jonathan [17], pp. 54–55.

[28] 482F.Supp741(S.D.N.Y.1980)affd623F.2d252(2dCir.1980).

4.2 Copying for Innovation Purpose

parody, but not whether the parody is a copy of the humor that the song itself already covers.

The idea that "copyright law" should include provisions that parody is applicable to critics has been criticized. Scholars worried that the judge offered too much leeway to the parodist and allowed them to infringe on copyright in the name of parody. Many different suggestions on the reform of parody pointed out that the extensive use of parody is unfair for rights holders, but those who hold this view ignored the premise that new creators can obtain valid authorization from the right holders. But in the case, the rights holder rejected the user's request through his monopoly position, and this rejection was not a factor that can be mediated through bargaining. "The parody defense has gone too far, which has led to now allowing blatant extortion of protected and valuable intellectual property." Posner emphasized that only a small number of parodies were required to obtain resources through authorization, so it should not be used as a defense against infringement. This was legal theft, and thieves were not privileged.

On the issue of parody, the application of the principle of fair use is not conducive to improving the consistency of judiciary and the predictability of legislation. It is very difficult to predict to what extent parodies can be accepted as fair use. These recommendations are based on the current system of fair use, and the different effects of judgments made on judges' discretion. From the perspective of the First Amendment to the Constitution, although commercial parody may become a behavior protected by the fair use system, its strong commercial interests place their copyright law framework in a questionable realm. In order to solve this problem, the law should encourage parody and encourage re-creation through minor changes, which will attract more people to engage in this form of creation, while also allowing copyright owners to profit from the parody market of others.

In practice, parody rarely has a negative impact on the market for rights holders. On the contrary, the success of certain "spoofs" has helped to increase people's demand for original works. In early 2006, the Internet-spoofing video "A blood bill caused by steamed bread" played a role in promoting the box office of the movie "The promise". Although this incident did not trigger actual litigation in the end, there was a climax of discussion in the academic world. This author believes that "A blood bill caused by steamed bread" itself does not fall into the scope of fair use, as the implied meaning of the short story to be conveyed by "steamed bread" has nothing to do with the movie "The Promise", and there is no deductive relationship between the "steamed bread" and the original work. And Hu Ge, the producer of "steamed bread", objectively did use the pictures in the movie "The Promise" to create and profited from it.[29] It is indeed a "free-rider", but the relationship between the two

---

[29] Although "A blood bill caused by steamed bread" was put on the Internet by right holder Hu Ge as a free resource for appreciation, the Internet economy did bring rewards to the author's creation,

works cannot be determined in the intellectual property system. In this case, we may try to consider it from the perspective of unfair competition. The rights holder of the movie "The Promise" should share part of the commercial benefits.

References

1. Cohen JE. The Place of the User in Copyright Law [J]. Fordham L. Rev., 2005, 74: 352
2. Liu Chuntian. Intellectual Property Law [M]. 4th ed. Beijing: China Renmin University Press, 2009: 75
3. Zheng Chengsi. Copyright Law (I) [M]. Beijing: China Renmin University Press, 2009: 181
4. Zhang Jin. Research on Private Copying in Copyright Law: From Printing Press to Internet [M]. Beijing: China University of Political Science and Law Press, 2009
5. Lohmannfy. Fair use as innovation policy [J]. Berkeley Technology Law Journal, 2008: 829
6. Feng Xiaoqing, Wei Yanliang. Modern Conflicts, Institutional Choices and Legal Philosophy Basis of Two types of Rights of Reproduction [M]//Peking University Intellectual Property Review (Vol. 2). Beijing: Law Press, 2004
7. William W. Fisher. Promises to Keep: Technology, Law, and the Future of Entertainment [M]. Li Xu, Trans. Shanghai: Shanghai Joint Publishing Press, 2008
8. Carla A. Hesse. The rise of intellectual property: An Idea in the Balance [J]. Jin Haijun, Zhong Xiaohong, Trans. Science-Technology and Law, 2007, 1. Original "The Rise of Intellectual Property, 700B.C.-AD2000: An Idea in the Balance" published in Daedalus (Spring 2002), pp. 26–45
9. Alfred D. Chandler, Jr., and James W. Cortada, eds. A nation transformed by information: How information has shaped the United States from colonial times to the present [M]. Wan Yan, Qiu Yanjuan. Shanghai: Shanghai Far East Publishers, 2008
10. John Gantz, Jack B. Rochester, Pirates of the Digital Millennium [M]. Zhou Xiaoqi, Trans. Beijing: Law Press, 2008: 22
11. John Howkins (2005) The Mayor's Commission on Creative Industries. In J. Hartley (ed.) Creative Industries. Oxford: Blackwell, 117–25
12. Howins (2001) The Creative Economy. London: Penguin
13. John Hartley. Creative Industries [M]. Cao Shule, BaoJiannv, Li Hui, Trans. Beijing: Tsinghua University Press, 2007
14. Kamina. Film Copyright in the European Union [M]. Ji Zhiwei, Yu Jianhong, Lin Xiaoxia, Trans. Beijing: China Film Press, 2006: 7–8
15. Lawrence Lessig. Free Culture [M]. Wangshi, Trans. Beijing: China CITIC Press, 2009: 73–76
16. Guo Liying. "Intertextuality" and "Parody" in the 20th Century Western Literature [J]. Journal of PLA University of Foreign Languages, 2003, 26(5)
17. Rosenoer Jonathan, Cyber Law [M]. Zhang Gaotong, et al. Trans. Beijing: China University of Political Science and Law Press, 2003
18. Ma Shuwei. The Parody in Modern Music [J]. Journal Of Guizhou University (Art Edition), 2005, 4(19)

---

such as his reputation and other business opportunities subsequently attracted by his talents. It is difficult to judge how much return Hu Ge has obtained from the spread of the "steamed bread" itself. At present, when the value does exist, the right holder can request a return for such use through a statutory license system. Regardless of whether the monetary value available to the ultimate right holder is high or low, at least this economic guarantee system reflects a respect for the interests of the original author.

Chapter 5
Reconstruction of the Rights Limitation System

If we never do anything which has not been done before, we shall never get anywhere. The law will stand still whilst the rest of the world goes on.[1] Legal norms and social norms are closely connected. Only when the law is consistent with social norms can it be recognized and respected by the public,[2] and can it work effectively. Therefore, the main task of the legislator is to identify and select reasonable social norms, to recognize them, and to give them legal effects.[3] By doing so, social governance can be achieved.

5.1 Impact of Digital Technology on Current Legal System

5.1.1 Digital Technology Eliminates Market Failures Caused by Excessively High Transaction Costs

In the field of copyright, whether there is market failure depends on the relationship between the rights holders and the users, and excessively high cost of obtaining authorization results in some space for users' "fair use". In a digital rights management ("DRM") system, rights holders do not need to specifically authorize someone to use their works under the fair use doctrine, and users do not need to go through various obstacles or visit each and every people that might be related to the rights. Inside a DRM system, the license and payment for the use of works can be achieved by simply exchanging some information and the transaction cost is no longer a barrier between rights holders and users.

---

[1] Denning [1]; quoted from the judgments of the *Packer v. Packer* case by Lord Denning, quoted from the preface to The Discipline of Law.

[2] Cooter [2].

[3] Basu [3] (The most important function of law is to select social norms, rather than to establish social norms).

© Intellectual Property Publishing House 2021
S. Liu, *Rights Limitation in Digital Age*,
https://doi.org/10.1007/978-981-16-4380-4_5

There are two types of market failure that the copyright law intends to solve: first, behaviors beyond control due to excessively high costs, such as private copying; and second, market inefficiency due to the monopoly formed in the copyright industry. In order to prevent the rights holder from monopolizing the market, copyright law adopts compulsory licensing, that is, regardless of whether the copyright owner consents, as long as the users fulfill the requirements stipulated by law, they can use the copyright owner's work upon payment of such use.[4]

Digital technology can solve the problem of market failure by recording and tracking the flow of digital information so that rights holders can know the use or spread of their works more accurately.

The preamble to the WIPO Copyright Treaty (WCT) stresses in particular that, in order to address the enormous challenges posed by the development of information and communication technologies, the contracting parties "recogniz[e] the profound impact of the development and convergence of information and communication technologies on the creation and use of literary and artistic work".[5] "Especially, information technology makes computer programs and databases possible, and information and communication technologies enable digital reproduction and transmission in various forms over digital networks. In addition, encryption technology and digital right information management are also very important for the use of works."[6]

First, digital technology is able to solve the problem in the traditional theory that the fair use system is established because of excessively high transaction costs.

Second, under the digital communication technology, disseminators obviously enjoy different status now as they begin to play a vital role in the actual dissemination of works. Under such circumstances, it is challenging to determine the "cost" in the dissemination of works. Because for dissemination through the new media, cost and benefit cannot be measured by treating works as commodities.

Involving cost in the dissemination of works is the premise of the transaction cost analysis method. However, in real life, transaction cost and benefit are gradually controlled by disseminators. Transaction cost is gradually decreasing with the development of technology, while benefit is increasing in a way that no longer relies on the reduction of dissemination cost. Cost and benefits are no longer two parameters that add up to zero, rather, benefit (by relying on factors other than technology) is now far higher than dissemination cost (which can be reduced directly by technology).

5.1.2 Trends in Social and Cultural Development Require the Continuation of the Fair Use System

Printing terminates the era of scribal culture and makes cross-cultural communication possible. To acquire knowledge and find books, scholars no longer need to

---

[4] Zhang and Lu [4], p. 17.

[5] World Intellectual Property Organization Copyright Treaty, WCT, 1996.

[6] Reinbert and von Lewinski [5].

5.1 Impact of Digital Technology on Current Legal System

travel around the world. Instead, they are able to sit in the library now and combine different ideological systems and professional disciplines. Furthermore, they are able to develop their minds and promote the combination of old ideas and new ideas by reviewing a rich variety of publications. In this "new era of cross-reference of books", a new ideological system is established.

Those who are both printers and scholars decide what kind of books will be in the library. With their advantages in ideological communication, printers attract scholars, literati and artists. The mode of printing technology changes cultural communication means that through the advancement of culture and the overturn of old ideas is brought by technological development. Therefore, it is of far-reaching significance to discuss the influence of the change of cultural communication, which is brought about by the technological revolution, on people's thoughts.

The relationship of cost and profit in the traditional publishing industry is like the two ends of a balance:

Income of [Author + disseminator (publisher, distributor, bookstore)] = expenditure of consumer.

Authors make literature and art a unique form of expression, and make it possible for this form of expression to be copyrighted. Booksellers, the first disseminators of books, do not have any legal standing in the civil law system on the ground that they are disseminators of intellectual property. In the scribal age, for booksellers, books are the same as rice or vases. Although the copyright system is established for the purpose of protecting the interests of the authors, "this system was not created with the birth of the first work, but was gradually developed after the widespread use of printing."[7] In this era, printers are also publishers, who make a contribution by providing scholars with a richer variety of books, which is far beyond the ability of book copying persons of the scribal age.[8]

In the Internet world, copyright-related stakeholders can be divided into three major interest groups: copyright owners who have rights to their works, Internet information disseminators represented by Internet service providers, and Internet information users represented by individual end users. However, with Internet becoming more and more influential, the boundaries among these three major interest groups are becoming blurred. Internet has reduced the cost of mass communication to a level that most people can afford. This makes new information sources of mass communication possible.[9] Compared with the high cost of starting a new newspaper or a radio station, one can start a personal radio station or create a digital magazine accessible from the Internet with just one computer, hardware devices that are accessible to the Internet, and some computer software.

"Personalized and typical new ideology may first enter the circle that printers and graphic artists are often in touch with. They publish clothing manuals, pattern books, royal commemorative albums and regional guides."[10] Therefore, although the *Statute*

---

[7] Zheng [6].

[8] Eisenstein [7], p. 42.

[9] Dominick [8].

[10] See Footnote 8.

of Anna was praised for its protection of "authors", what we see behind said authors are publishers. When publishers were separated from printers, not only do they get profits from publishing, but also the jacket of authors. At the very beginning, talented and creative scholars and artists not only worked on reprinting old books, but they themselves might be publishers. Since the 16th century, the most advanced academic centers seemed to have moved from lecture halls and teaching centers to printers' workshops. Printers need to constantly consult professors, painters, translators, plate dealers, chief librarians, etc. before a work is published.[11] Printers play the important role of leading the culture development. They control symbols and influence people's understanding of the world.

In the era when ideas were spread by manuscript, the sorting of speeches, classroom scripts, texts, poems, etc. into books that meet printing requirements was creation itself. "Fair use" came into being with the birth of the copyright system, and works were created by the reorganizing of existing materials. "Property rights, in the form of a system coat, cover the social relations that are full of historical and cultural contingency and have undergone various changes and combinations over time."[12] Under the digital context, the fair use system needs to find its position in the new era, and at the same time to maintain its standing in the traditional copyright system for the purpose of public interests.

5.2 Establishment of Digital Rights Management Systems

5.2.1 Digital Rights Management

5.2.1.1 Definition

DRM systems refers to the technical means by which rights holders control and protect copyrighted works using digital technologies. DRM systems are designed to make infringement hard to achieve and costly. In order to monopolize the rights to works, rights holders have been making various efforts using digital technology. For example, at the very beginning, copyrights holders of musical works tried to prevent the copying of works by encrypting records and CDs, but this appeared to have little effect. A relatively successfully approach is implemented via Internet to prevent loss resulted from infringement. This approach is able to effectively control the use of data by disseminators and end users.

---

[11] See Footnote 8.

[12] Yu [9].

5.2 Establishment of Digital Rights Management Systems

5.2.1.2 Functions

(1) Communication

The most important role of printing is its function of storage[13], while the most important contribution that digital technology has made is through its function of communication. Before 2000, most people purchased music CDs. The record industry controls the music market. After 2000, with the development of the music digitization technology, a music file format similar to the effect of CDs has become more and more popular. Apple's iTunes music store came into being at that time. It was a time when unauthorized music works can be downloaded from the Internet very easily. The music industry blames the infringement "disaster" for its declining in the following years. While users who were used to download pirated music ridiculed Apple for its paid music services, they soon found that free music resources would no longer be so easily available. During that transition period, Apple quickly grasped nearly 70% of the online music download market share. iTunes becomes a successful DRM platform that is run on "fair payment".

(2) Recording the use of rights

The deployment of DRM mechanisms will solve many problems that have been difficult for the traditional systems. First, as mentioned above, the circumstances that cause market failure no longer exist. Second, DRM systems also allow fair use for the purpose of public interests. In the digital world, when all transactions can be accurately calculated, does the copyright system need to limit the rights holders using the fair use doctrine? The author's answer is no. The rights holders can now control everything, and the amount of profits that they would obtain can be completely left to the market. Fair use is the limitation on rights holder in the interests of users. However, when rights holders are able to or uses other means to obtain more profits, it is no longer necessary to provide users with space for fair use. Under such circumstances, the rights holders have voluntarily given up obtaining profits using the traditional method, which relies heavily on the original works. This is a balancing of what to "give up" and what to "pursue".

5.2.1.3 Impact on the Rights Limitation System

It is somewhat flawed to rely solely on computer calculations to measure fair use. For example, such calculation may not be able to identify situations in which a small number of copyrighted works are used for re-creation. In many specific cases, whether the re-creation of copyrighted works is fair use is a huge challenge for judges. For rights holders, the fair use doctrine is not welcomed, though it is the warmly welcomed doctrine when rights holders engage in creative activities. How to strike a balance from the legal perspective is challenging? There is no precedent for

---

[13] Eisenstein [7], p. 67.

a proper measurement of fair use, especially in the United States where the doctrine of "sweat of the brow" is applied.[14]

It is not easy to persuade the rights holders to establish a system that may absolve the users' behavior in order to protect users' fair use rights. As is with the non-digital technology environment, one might receive a Lawyer Letter even for the use of a music background of only a few seconds. There are more and more conflicts in reality, such as the protracted disputes in the "Dancing Baby" case. At the same time of preventing rights holders from abusing their absolute rights, it is necessary to prohibit video platforms from disseminating fragmented works in order to avoid risks. Such behavior is infringement in the disguise of fair use.

To encourage fair use in the digital technology environment, both rights holders and users expect that law and technology can solve problems caused by using works in the digital technology environment.

Under this new paradigm, end users should be given more flexibility to use digital contents. For example, the future DRM mechanisms may have, from the perspective of information dissemination, the function of allowing authorization from several data sources, including data sources of end users. It can, based on the traditional rights theory, design a fair use right that aims at defined end users. It is recommended that the traditional DRM system be expanded so that authorization can be obtained from difference sources, including from end users. This will be helpful for rights holders to control the use of their works.

In the field of copyright, the distinction between public and private is not always clear cut. It is highly possible that what people watch, listen, and read is a mixture of publicly and privately produced content. In many cases, people have difficulty distinguishing between the two. For example, news programs produced by BBC are often broadcasted by commercial TV stations.[15]

In the fair use system, the purpose of almost all the actions listed therein is to eventually create new social wealth, including both material and spiritual wealth. Other than for re-creation purposes, all other use of copyrighted works listed in the statute, including criticism, comment, news reporting, and teaching, can be converted into a part of labour value (ie, their cost can be calculated). Within the framework of the current copyright law, we may take "limitations on copyright" as the starting point, and put "statutory license" and "fair use" in parallel. Then, we may try to expand the scope of statutory license, and strictly restrict the application of the fair use doctrine.

5.2.2 Temporary Reproduction

Under the new technology, special attention should be paid to the nature of temporary reproduction and the conflicts of interests it brings. It is necessary for us to define what

---

[14] F10 by Timothy K. Armstrong.

[15] Hartley [10], p. 13.

5.2 Establishment of Digital Rights Management Systems

kind of "personal use" is fair use. When the requirements for fair use are met, is it still necessary to defend on the ground of "fair use"? This author believes that the answer is no. The premise of any personal use should be that when a user obtains, enjoys, or uses a work, he is a consumer of the work and has paid a fair consideration for his private use, and the copyright owner has obtained his work-based property profits. The act of "enjoying" a copyrighted work without paying a fair consideration shall be regarded as "non-fair" use and constitutes an infringement. People can sometimes find the latest and most popular movies on video sites, especially a large number of Chinese websites. Those sites provide some Hollywood blockbusters with Chinese subtitles translated by different translation entities. In the titles of those films, we can always find statements used as "disclaimers", such as "for personal use only", or "please delete after downloading".

From 2003 to 2008, in the 8385 copyright and neighboring right cases in China, 87 involve "fair use", accounting for only 1.04% of the total. The difference in the number of cases around the country clearly reveals regional differences.[16] Both public awareness on copyright and rights holders' awareness to protect their rights are increasing. However, although the number of cases related to copyrights has been increasing year by year, the number of cases involving "fair use" has not increased accordingly. On the contrary, the occurrence of such cases is becoming less frequent.

As mentioned above, since its birth, intellectual property system has become a instrument for capital operators who claim to be authors to achieve great economic benefits. We are not criticizing this system. As not only do authors and inventors benefit from this system spiritually and materially, publishers and manufacturers also obtain economic benefits through monopoly of rights as well. All entities in this system has obtained what they need and maximized their interests. This is a macro level economic balance. However, there are now people who would rather give up this right and maximize their interests by other means.

The Digital Millennium Copyright Act ("DMCA") is an amendment to ensure longer-term protection of interest groups. 10 years after its adoption, the most valuable companies in the United States that rely heavily on digital technology development gave up their "exclusive rights" and used means such as the open source approach to obtain greater profits. In 2011, Apple Inc. ranked third among the Global 500 companies released by *Financial Times*, with 100 technology companies in the list. In 2012, in the Global 500 companies released by *Fortune*, an authoritative magazine in the US, the ranking of Apple Inc. went up from the 111th in the previous year to the 55th.[17] Although the above two data seem to be very different, which is largely because their evaluation parameters are different, it is undeniable that Apple Inc. has become the most dazzling star due to its performance in recent years.

Legal norms should be rooted in social activities, and we should understand the "law in daily life" from social, cultural, economic and political perspectives, rather than limiting the scope of research to law (statutes, or precedent or judgments) itself,

---

[16] Zhang and Lu [4], p. 165.

[17] Key words search from Baidu.com by "global 500 companies in 2012". [EB/OL]. http://baike. baidu.com/view/8958857.htm.

i.e., the "law in the books". This can help with the achieving the purpose of the legal-social analysis.

Although the copyright law explicitly gives users the right of fair use, when copyrighted works are in digital form, fair use is no longer possible. Copyright owners are beginning to establish the DRM system. In this system, each use by the user will require permission from the rights holder, or payment of corresponding consideration for the use. Rights holders now have unprecedented control of the use of their works. Although there are always technically skilled people who can figure out ways to bypass the DRM control system, in the United States, this behavior might violate the DMCA. The rights controller of copyright can effectively evade "fair use" through the digital rights system, thus protecting its income. Further, as the DMCA gives rights holders the legal guarantee to limit fair use, this may result in the possibility of reduced users' exercising of their legally protected rights. As more and more copyrighted works appear in digital form, one cannot help but ask whether the DRM mechanism will end the era when users are free to use protected works in accordance with the law. The DRM system may reduce the differences in reality caused by statutory license and technical capabilities. The fair use system will have new scope of application in the new technical environment. In the future, the DRM system will play a role of adjusting the relationship between rights holders and users, rather than simply eliminating fair use.

5.2.3 Legal Liabilities of Network Operators

As an important knowledge disseminator in the knowledge economy, network operators are expecting to become publishers in the traditional intellectual property system. Further, their role in knowledge dissemination is far different from those who work in the traditional media industry. Therefore, when we try to reconstruct the system of limitations on copyright, the legal liabilities of network operators should be considered. Strengthening the liabilities of the online media will further protect the interests of rights holders, and will greatly impact the profits allocation to rights holders during statutory license.

People who provide Internet services include Internet content providers and Internet service providers, who are responsible for providing Internet related contents and hardware services, respectively. According to the "28th Statistical Report on China's Internet Development" released by China Internet Network Information Center (CNNIC), as of June 2011, the number of Chinese Internet users was 485 million. Taking the use of digital music as an example, in the first half of 2011, the number of online music users was 382 million and the usage rate was 78.7%, second only to the use of search engines and instant messaging. However, the number of users who actually pay for music downloading is small. To change this situation, we should first have a look at the legal liabilities of network operators.

5.2 Establishment of Digital Rights Management Systems

5.2.3.1 Internet Content Providers

Internet content providers (ICP) is the entity who selects certain types of information and uploads it on the Internet for users to access. Anyone can be an ICP, whether it being a individual user or a large enterprise, as long as it posts information on the Internet. If there is illegal or infringing content in the uploaded information, the copyright owner can sue ICP and ask them to bear the liabilities for posting such content.[18]

Taking digital music as an example, in recent years, there are many infringement lawsuits against Internet service providers, including websites such as Baidu, Sogou and Thunder. These lawsuits are protracted and costly, but nothing significant has been achieved. In the lawsuits filed by record companies against Baidu and Yahoo, record companies are awarded compensation that merely covers the losses that they suffered. As the principle adopted by the Chinese intellectual property system is that the damages awarded shall cover the losses, the costs of infringements are low. This does not serve the ultimate purpose of promoting a music industry that encourages the use of authorized music and prohibits the use of pirated music. In an Internet environment where legal protection is weak, consumers have become used of obtaining copyrighted works free of charge.

5.2.3.2 Internet Service Provider

An Internet Service Provider ("ISP") is the person who provides information communication intermediary service via the Internet. An ISP transmits or receives information based merely on users' choice, and does not review or filter the disseminated information. As a medium for the transmission of information over the Internet, an ISP's computer system or other device stores and transmits information.[19] Therefore, when a rights holder discovers an infringement, the ISP shall bear the corresponding liabilities. Digital music is illegally disseminated via the Internet, and there are various ways to access music, as long as you have access to the Internet. People can obtain digital music from various channels, for example, deep-link websites, illegal music search engines, music audio-visual websites providing infringing or pirated music, point-to-point services, music boxes, cloud storage services or audio-visual Internet disks, and Internet radio stations. Such loose intellectual property protection environment in China makes music piracy very easy, with the cost of infringement extremely low. Other countries had had such problems too. Some countries have succeeded in curbing Internet infringement acts by legislations that respond to digital technology and by establishing a stern judicial environment.

Technically speaking, ISPs in China are able to block pornographic and politically controversial content through various means. Rather than filtering the users of individual websites, the "Great Firewall" of China filters by blacklisted keywords,

---

[18] Song [11].

[19] Xue [12].

and network operators block the traffic of bad information by filtering by keywords. Therefore, it is technically feasible to block infringement use. There is no specific legal provision in China that determines the infringement liabilities of an ISP. Article 57 of the Regulations on Telecommunications of the People's Republic of China (the "Telecommunications Regulations") provides eight specific situations under which no organization or individual may use telecommunications network to produce, reproduce, disseminate or transmit information. Intellectual property rights are not involved in those situations. However, in the catch-all provisions of Article 57.9, it is stipulated that no content that is prohibited by laws or administrative regulations may be implemented. Similar as the Telecommunications Regulations, the Regulations on Internet Information Services of the People's Republic of China does not have clauses that specifically address intellectual property protection. Although the above provisions can be applied to pirate behavior, it is difficult to find a specific system or clause to determine ISP liabilities, either in judicial practice or in the entire intellectual property protection system.

5.2.3.3   Safe Harbor Principle and Red Flag Standard

The safe harbor principle says that when a copyright infringement occurs, for ISPs who only provides space and does not create web content, they should delete the infringing content upon notice of infringement, otherwise they will be determined as infringing. If the infringing content is neither stored on an ISP's server nor is the ISP informed of what content to delete, the ISP does not commit infringement. This principle is later applied to search engines, Internet storage, online libraries and so on. The safe harbor principle consists of two processes, i.e., notice and takedown. As a principle against the safe harbor principle, the red flag standard means that under the following two circumstances, an information storage space and information location service provider will not bear secondary infringing liabilities due to other's direct infringement: (1) the provider is "not actually aware of" the content uploaded by a user or the content that a link leads up to is infringing, and (2) while "in the absence of the actual awareness state", the provider is also not aware of the facts or circumstances that indicate apparent infringing acts.[20] When the facts and circumstances of infringement by others is blatantly flying like a red flag in front of an ISP, to an extent that rational people in the same situation are aware of, the ISP that pretends to have not seen the fact of infringing acts by takes the "ostrich" policy should be determined as at least "should be aware of" the infringing acts.

Both the DMCA of the United States and the *Regulations on the Protection of the Rights of Communication through Information Network* of China involve the safe harbor principle and the red flag standard. The red flag standard has been applied in judicial practices of China.[21] In both foreign and domestic precedents, the premise for the prioritized use of the safe harbor principle is that the infringer has not "induced

---

[20] Wang [13].

[21] *UnionVoole v. TCL and Thunder.*

5.2 Establishment of Digital Rights Management Systems

infringement". That is, when an infringement is resulted from the specific business model of an operator, the safe harbor principle will not apply.[22] Determination of such wrong doings is beyond the red flag standard. This trend of judicial practice reflects that the law is responding to the new problems brought by technological development so as to apply the safe harbor principle in a stricter manner.

For the current Internet companies, the boundaries between ICP and ISP have become increasingly blurred. Except for telecommunication companies that only provide transmission services, Internet service providers that provide only storage services have gradually become content providers. Especially, with the development of cloud technologies, the two are unifying as one. The safe harbor principle has not played a positive role in the current intellectual property legal system in China, instead, it has become a real "safe harbor" for infringement. As the current intellectual property system in China adopts the principle of compensation rather than indemnity, infringers may use the safe harbor principle as a protection for its infringing acts. In a jurisdiction environment where the cost of infringement is extremely low and the cost of rights defending is excessively high, the use of the safe harbor principle is against the justice that law intents to protect.

5.2.3.4 "Three Strikes" Law

The American Recording Industry Association first proposed that it wishes to use the advantages of ISPs and cooperate with them in order to realize the protection of rights. This mechanism of cooperation is called "two strikes". That is, when users infringe on the copyright of others by illegally sharing files, ISPs are in the position to warn users that their services would be cut down if they continue to do so.[23] South Korea began to crack down on piracy by implementing the "three strikes" in 2009, and has achieved great success. The occurrence of illegal downloads drops sharply, and the income from digital music increase greatly. Under such a mechanism, creators will be greatly motivated.[24] Although the introduction of "three strikes" was originally aimed at point-to-point file sharing, the mechanism has played a significant role in combating the current music piracy in China. At the same time, the adding of the liabilities of telecommunications service providers to the copyright system plays a positive role both in implementing statutory license in the rights limitation system, and in protecting the economic interests of rights holders.

The "three strikes" mechanism has aroused hot debates during its implementation in different countries. ISPs' rights to terminate the use of terminals by users violate privacy and freedom of speech. However, countries that have implemented the "three strikes" mechanism can now better protect their copyright, and such protection is good for public interests.

---

[22] See Footnote 20.

[23] Song [14].

[24] IFPI. Digital Music Report 2011.

Different from the situation in China, in countries where copyright are well protected, it is very difficult to find free music resources from ICP's services. Rights holders in other countries are more concerned about the spread of copyrighted works through point-to-point software. "Three strikes" are mainly targeted at such infringement. Most countries add this mechanism to their legislations in the past few years. Besides South Korea mentioned above, the Taiwan region of China implemented said legislation from April 2009, France from September 2009, and New Zealand from September 2011. This phenomenon shows that "three strikes" is a powerful measure with regard to technological reform, and that countries have responded to the upset of balance brought by technological development in the post-industrial era by timely amending their laws.

This author believes that it is necessary to add the mechanism of "three strikes" to the Chinese legal system, as this principle will help purify the legal environment of Internet intellectual property. With regard to the widespread use and dissemination of pirated works on the Internet in China, "three strikes" is a solution that can fix the problem "in one step". Its establishment would not only impose the strictest constraints on ICPs, but also will it provide a fair competition environment for Internet service providers. Further, it would improve the profitability of Internet companies.

5.3 Statutory License

5.3.1 Definition and Function of Statutory License

Copyright law shall address the market failures in the following two cases: first, behaviors beyond control due to excessively high costs, such as private copying; second, market inefficiency due to the monopoly power shaped by the copyright industry. To prevent copyright owners from monopolizing the market, the copyright license adopts compulsory license (statutory license), that is, regardless of whether the copyright owner consents, as long as the users fulfill the requirements stipulated by law, they can use the copyright owner's work upon payment of such use.[25]

The statutory license system and the fair use system are two different limitations on rights in the copyright limitation system. Both of them are based on the premise that the rights holder's permission is not required. The difference lies in whether they require remuneration to the rights holder.

---

[25] Zhang and Lu [4], p. 171.

5.3.2 Legislation in Some Countries

5.3.2.1 United States

The US statutory license system is mainly embodied in the following three aspects: anti-monopoly, market pricing, and public interest-based protection of the public's right to know.[26]

It is generally believed that the system of limitations on the copyright mainly consists of three parts: fair use, statutory license (applicable for legally authorized people who use the work of others within a certain range without the permission of the copyright owner), and compulsory license (applicable for people who are qualified to apply for the right to use the work of others with competent authority).

According to the legislation and amendment history of the US copyright law on statutory license, with the advancement of technology, changes of reproduction conditions brought about by the new replication technology directly affects the scope of rights limitations within the copyright system. For example, with temporary reproduction of certain sound recordings gaining statutory license in 1998, a new balance aimed at protecting the public's access right to protected works was achieved.

The US copyright law provides several statutory licenses, including statutory licenses that allow:

(a)   secondary cable transmissions (section 111);
(b)   certain public broadcasting and retransmission of sound recordings and works (section 114);
(c)   making and distributing phonorecords of nondramatic musical works (section 115);
(d)   use of nondramatic musical works in sound recordings and works by coin-operated phonorecord players (section 116);
(e)   use of published nondramatic musical works, and published pictorial, graphic, and sculptural works in non-commercial broadcasting (section 118);
(f)   retransmission of super stations and internet stations, with private families being the audience (the Satellite Home Viewers Act enacted in 1988);
(g)   temporary reproduction of certain sound recordings (DMCA);
(h)   satellite broadcasting in the original market (the Satellite Home Viewers Act, as amended in 1999).

5.3.2.2 Germany

German Act on Copyright and Related Rights has the following principled provisions on statutory license:

①   Article 46 provides that reproduction and distribution shall be permissible where limited parts of works, of works of language and of musical works, individual

---

[26] Li and Cao [15].

works of fine art are incorporated after their publication in a collection which is intended, by its nature, exclusively for religious, school or instructional use.

② Article 47 provides that schools and institutions for the training and further training of teachers may make individual copies of works which are included in a school broadcast by recording the works on a video or audio medium. The video or audio recordings may be used only for instructional purposes. They must be destroyed not later than the end of the school year following the transmission of the school broadcast, unless equitable remuneration has been paid to the author.

③ Article 49.1 provides that it shall be permissible to reproduce and distribute individual broadcast commentaries and individual articles from newspapers and other information journals devoted solely to issues of the day in other newspapers or journals of like kind and to communicate such commentaries and articles to the public, if they concern political, economic or religious issues of the day and do not contain a statement reserving rights.

④ Article 54 provides that where the nature of a work is such that it may be expected to be reproduced by the recording of broadcasts on video or audio recording mediums or by transfer from one recording medium to another, the author of the work shall be entitled to payment of equitable remuneration from the manufacturers or importers of video or audio recording mediums for such reproduction. Claims to remuneration shall be asserted through a collecting society.[27]

In addition, Article 61 details the reproduction of sound recordings.

5.3.2.3 Canada

As a Commonwealth country, Canada's copyright law system is similar to that of the United Kingdom. The fair dealing provisions in the Canadian copyright law are roughly the same as those stipulated by other countries. "Fair dealing" is limited to the sole purpose of private study, criticism, review and news reporting.[28] However, the fair dealing provisions may apply on purposes other than research or private study if the source of the copied work can be proved.

Bill C-11, which was passed in Canada in 2011, has a great impact on academic institutions. Some scholars believe that excessive protection of works is an exception to private use and research under the fair dealing provisions...Bill C-11 provides protection for copyrighted materials with "digital locks" based on the DRM system. This measure will have a negative impact on the research and learning rights of academic institutions and result in increased costs to obtain information for educational institutions and students. However, scholars holding opposite opinion believe that "each year, a large amount of materials are copied and used for teaching purposes

---

[27] Hu [16].

[28] Article 29 of the Canadian Copyright Act.

5.3 Statutory License 97

in Canada, and some of these are not paid a penny." "If major markets like academic institutions do not have to follow copyright policy and pay royalties, authors will not obtain any economic support to carry out their work. Therefore, the exceptions under the fair dealing provisions will further hinder publication."[29]

Excessively loose conditions for the application of fair dealing by the academic institutions might make the management of education and academia even harder. Finding shared interests between academic institutions and academic research authors is what needs to be solved under the digital background. Although the "digital lock" method increases the cost of academic researchers to obtain materials, the Internet actually eliminates the restrictions on obtaining academic materials using traditional methods. Students and teachers are no longer constrained by the lack of library materials when conducting related research, or by the limit of time in obtaining materials. From this perspective, it is reasonable to pay corresponding costs for the convenience of the Internet. In fact, in this process, the exception of traditional fair dealing is reverted to authorized use. However, the reverting may also bring with it a stronger pricing position to the copyright owner. In order to seek a balance of interests, a third party needs to be involved. If academic institutions continue to be exempted from paying remunerations, public interest will eventually be harmed even if the starting point is to protect public interest, unless someone is willing to fund the development of academic publishing.

5.4 Restructuring of the System of Copyright Limitations

The fair use doctrine was originally directed at those highly controllable transmission resources. The use of such resources is based on the transfer of property rights. However, the advent of the Internet has made it possible for resources to be transmitted to any place at any time. Whoever finds it can use it. Hence, the concept of fair use has become completely different.

According to John Gonz and Jack Rochester, DMCA subtly restrains the fair use system through its provisions on copyright protection and encryption. Although fair use of content is permitted by law, due to encryption and other measures, it may be extremely difficult for users to obtain a fragment from a work, especially from musical or audio-visual works. Of course, the users can ask the rights holder for permission to obtain the part they want to use, but this will return to the two possibilities of fair use. If it comes to imitation or comment, the rights holder is only willing to authorize people who give positive evaluation, which means the space for fair use by those that give negative evaluation will become even smaller. If people no longer enjoy the right of "fair use", or when the exercise of the fair use right is objectively impossible, will this system still be meaningful? Allowing others to use

---

[29] "The New Canadian Copyright Act May Cause Negative Effects", from the website of China Intellectual Property Protection [EB/OL]. http://www.ipr.gov.cn/guojiiprarticle/guojiipr/guobiehj/gbhjnews/201110/1262623_1.html.

a small part of the work can encourage creativity and bring the rights holder new benefits, which is what the rights holders would like to see. When the rights holders are the artists themselves, they may be even more tolerant of fair use. Which factor plays a part in the above, the fair use system or the giving up of the rights by the rights holders? Obviously, the answer is the latter. In this way, the status of fair use will be even more instable, and its role in the entire copyright system will become weaker and weaker.

In this author's opinion, during the amending of copyright law, fair use does not need to be meticulous, on the contrary, it should be presented in a principled way in the law. When the rights holder gives up the realization of some rights in exchange for other rewards, fair use does not have to serve as a weapon for the user to break through the limits of rights.

5.4.1 Strictly Limit the Scope of Fair Use

In the context of new technologies, it is possible to effectively improve on the situation where the rights holder cannot make a profit due to transaction costs under fair use. Thus, the application of fair use can be limited, while the scope of statutory license can be expanded.

In the two circumstances of market failure, what conclusive factors can be the ruling for fair use? The answers can be found in the following cases. In *American Geophysical Union's v. Texaco Inc.*, the court decides that Texaco's unauthorized photocopying of articles in scientific journals does not constitute fair use. In *Princeton University Press v. Michigan Document Services, Inc.*, the court rejected the claim that the photocopy shop should give its sales profit to a professor at the University of Michigan as it is fair use.

The above two cases mainly focus on the fourth factor in section 107 of the US Copyright Law, "the effect of use upon the potential market for or value of copyrighted work". The Copyright Settlement Center of the American Geophysical Union provides a way for users to obtain authorization; while Princeton Press sets up a separate authority department. These make the court believe that obtaining a license to use a work through a tool is a technical measure by the rights holder to avoid economic loss, and whatever work restricted by this measure should be protected. The court reasoned that the loss of copyright fees constituted a fact that the market was damaged, and Judge Newman announced to the American Geophysical Union that "a particular unauthorized use should be considered 'more fair' when there is no ready market or means to pay for the use, while such an unauthorized use should be considered 'less fair' when there is a ready market or means to pay for the use." This requires users to be legally authorized in a feasible way.

The reasons that the scope of fair use should be strictly restricted include:

1. Fair use is not conducive to protecting the author's right to claim remuneration. The *Campbell v. Acuff-Rose Music* case reveals that the legality of fair use means

5.4 Restructuring of the System of Copyright Limitations

that even if the user has applied for authorization and was rejected, his use is legal. The rights holder of the song has refused to authorize "2LiveCrew" to adapt the song, but the court assumed that the doctrine of fair use is applicable here as the new song contains parody commenting on and criticizing of the original work. However, in such circumstances where users' success is based on the original work, they do not need to share the revenue with the original author. This reduces the rights holder's chance to obtain additional profit.

2. Fair use also means that the rights holder will not be compensated for the use of others. Under such circumstance, the work seems to have nothing to do with the rights holder. One can imagine a system in which any user can find and use anything they want, as long as they pay remuneration to the rights holder for their use. Fair use is not equivalent to statutory license. A fair remuneration mechanism shall be established for rights holders.

3. Most users are anonymous as fair use requires neither authorization nor payment. Compared with actively seeking rights holders to obtain authorization of use, they prefer to meet their own needs anonymously. However, in this way, rights holders will always keep an eye on whether their works are unreasonably "fair-used" to prevent damage to their interests. Obviously, in the traditional environment, rights holders have little means to restrict users' "fair use". However, in the digital environment, the status of users and rights holders may reverse. The rights holders can now control the use of all their works. It becomes impossible for those users who neither need to obtain authorization nor pay the necessary remuneration to continue to use the rights holders' works anonymously. In the digital age, a new imbalance has formed between the two interest groups, with the rights holder being the dominant party.[30]

5.4.2 Expanding the Scope of Statutory License

Scarcity in the market is the premise of any transaction. In the traditional market of works, transactions for acquiring knowledge need an object, such as a book, a painting, a record, etc. Rights holders can protect their own interests by controlling the transaction of copies, At one time, digital technology broke this balance, and countries correspond to the changes by formulating laws aimed at strengthening the protection of rights. Today, however, the balance tilted once again towards rights holders due to the DRM technology. In a market where scarcity is established again, rights holders can resort to the DRM technology to realize stronger monopoly. Once again, the balance of interests is broken. Therefore, the law now needs to be amended to better protect the public interest.

Different from the traditional system where rights holders control the behavior of "copying", the most dangerous outcome from the monopoly of digital technology is that, rights holders will control the user's behavior of "use". For example, no one knows how many people have "used" the old magazines in the barber shop. The

---

[30] Timothy K. Armstrong.

writer of a magazine does not care about and cannot control the circulation after the magazine is sold. What they can control is the copies of the magazine out of which they earn their remunerations according to the sales volume. By technical means under the condition of DRM, the rights holders can prevent users from copying and can know the use or spread of their works more accurately than ever before. Besides, they can use the data, including the frequency of use, time, location and users etc. to determine users' preferences, develop new business models according to the using habits of specific groups, and earn more profits.

Users are in a relatively weak position, and have to obtain authorization to gain access to relevant knowledge. To be authorized, they must pay the corresponding consideration, which is based on their capacity to pay. Excessively high monopoly rights will harm the public's access right. Therefore, in some fields, the aggressive monopoly position of the rights holder should be weakened, and statutory license should be adopted instead. This can not only protect the economic rights of rights holders, but also maximize the effective use of knowledge.

Regarding the reprinting of written works, the proviso clause in Article 32 of the Copyright Law, which says that "the copyright owner has declared that reprinting or excerpting is not permitted", shall be removed. Because this regulation does not play a positive role in disseminating works. Rather, it limits the scope of the statutory license. In the context of digital technology, this proviso clause are often invalid and fails to provide rights holders with the security of authorizing others to use, let alone harming the rights holders' economic interests.

5.4.3 Business Transformation Achieved by Strict Rights Limitations and Strong Rights Protections

Highly monopolized control does not impede the development of creativity. Rather, it provides a secure market environment for new business models and encourages enterprises to create new profit models.

5.4.3.1 Open Source

Take computer software for example, from the initial stage of this industry to the beginning of the 21st century, the source code of software has remained the core intellectual property for software companies. However, with the development of technology, the function of software is no longer limited to spying on the source code of software, and the cost of independently developing software is greatly reduced. Over the past few years, new mainstream software companies have changed their protection strategies for software source code. Take Apple Inc. for example, having its source code public does not cause infringement on its software, instead, it shortens the cycle for program development and inspires the creativity of programmers.

5.4 Restructuring of the System of Copyright Limitations

Neither information technology nor code is the primary driving force of economic activity any longer. People are interested in ideas and knowledge, not information; they are interested in experience, not just continuity. In the 1980s, most computer companies strained the veil of mystery and called for legislation to deal with piracy and hacking. But 20 years later, the most profitable software design companies are making their source code public to users so that users can download on their own and independently develop the functions on the software platform by themselves.

The original intention of making source code public was to make the code of computer program publicly available so that all users could see and use it to develop new software.[31] Open source is a design feature, and it enables the involvement of more people in the Internet and the rapid development of the Internet. For some people, open source is a technical means; for some others, it is a hobby; for yet a lot more others, it is a social movement and a blueprint for economic and social development.[32] Creativity requires some space of "free use". While owning a copyright can add value and promote creativity, and give rewards and incentives to rights holders, it limits the use of the creativity by others. When the new economic model develops to a certain stage, the distribution of interests to all parties will reach a balance. In fact, the intent to design a system is to ensure the balance of interests. The practice of open source is a breakthrough of the current copyright system. By making the source code public, right holders give up part of their interests, and attract more entity to join in the innovation. Thus, they are able to get more profits. When the new economy is about imagination, knowledge and creativity, a new development framework will emerge correspondingly.[33] In this new economic model, a reasonable design will affect the balance of interests of all parties.

The practice of making source code public by computer software companies is not only a business behavior that can quickly attracts users and reduces the cost of later development, but also a challenge to the current system of intellectual property right.

In fact, "we media" has emerged in the open and new publishing environment, with many Internet users uploading their own works to literary websites and sharing others' works with other users. It is often free to read or download works, although users have to pay for surfing online.

5.4.3.2 New Applications of the Traditional Business Model

Strictly speaking, sharing benefits with rights holders is not something new. Since the establishment of the intellectual property system, the disseminators of works have been sharing benefits with authors. However, in the digital age, a new approach to facilitating market transactions, expanding wealth, and generating profits is established with the development of technology.

---

[31] Wikepedia, Open Source [EB/OL]. http://zh.wikipedia.org/zh-cn/opencode.

[32] Hartley [10], p. 36.

[33] See Footnote 32.

The success of Apple Inc. is a typical example. With the launch of Apple's iPod in 2001, Apple's stock valuation increased sevenfold. This increase is directly attributable to the success of iPod. However, the success is not merely a success of a hardware device, nor a success in the market share of the MP3 player. Apple Inc. owes its success to its business model in which it shares the sales revenue with the rights holders, allowing more users to use the copyrighted works at a relatively low price. The upsurge of MP3 player also gave birth to the aftermarket. According to the data as of 2006, the aftermarket of MP3 player had exceeded 200 million US dollars. The new business model and accessory products increasingly demand an effective legal environment. Taking the sales volume of musical works as an example, the annual major albums released in terms of physical units dropped rapidly from US $12.9 billion in 2001 to US $900 million in 2008.It may be difficult to determine the reasons objectively, but part of the reason for this rapid decline in revenue can be attributed to private copying, for example, using iPods to obtain and enjoy music. However, with such type of electronic storage, only a small proportion of works were initially downloaded in a legitimate way. This leads to a variety of piracy. In recent years, with many countries actively amending their laws, digital works are more and more effectively protected. Besides, Apple Inc.'s business model has given rise to many new forms of economic activity, and its success has prompted Apple to have a determination to continue to grow its iTunes business, which has maximized returns to the company. This business model extends from music sharing to APP sharing, from music storage to the application in mobile phones and laptops, to meet the needs of more users anytime and anywhere.

We have to admit that successful business models are inseparable from sound legal environment. There are still many problems in the traditional field of intellectual property protection in China. This means that intellectual property protection in a digital environment is challenging. Despite the rapid development of the digital economy over the past decade, many domestic Internet enterprises still haven't found a business model that can generate profit based on copyrighted works. This is mainly due to the relatively poor legal environment of intellectual property rights in China. Since this situation is affected by many factors, such as legislation, judicial practices, law enforcement and legal awareness, it is necessary to start from legislation and consolidate the legal system so as to fit in the digital technology environment.

5.4.4 Establishing a "Fair Use" Welfare System Rooted in the Public Law System

The doctrine of fair use provides space for economic innovation, and encourages technology companies to invest in and establish new markets. But, is it appropriate to treat fair use as a country's policy for innovation? It is very likely that rights holders will oppose to this. If so, should we set up a remuneration mechanism to provide

5.4 Restructuring of the System of Copyright Limitations

space for innovative companies or individuals to legally obtain authorization from copyright owner?

(1)   Formulating a compulsory licensing system in the form of administrative law

Copyright compulsory license is a legal system in which the copyright authority grants the person who applies for the right to use the published work under specific conditions. Due to the nature of the public law, the author believes that the system decided by the administrative intervention should be independent of the copyright system so as to protect the public interest. We can refer to the provisions of the current foreign copyright law on obtaining protected works for vulnerable groups, such as translating the copyrighted works for those who are visually impaired to acquire knowledge; translating some copyrighted works to maintain and protect the cultural rights of ethnic minorities (in this case a lower standard of payment obligation shall be assumed, and the cost shall be paid by the national finance of the region where the minority language is used).

(2)   Imposing additional taxes on the increasing profits of rights holders

The amendments of law aim to balance the interests of the parties which are constantly changing. Under the condition of strict limitations on rights in both legislation and judicial practices, at the same time of expanding the scope of rights holders' monopoly rights and economic returns, a country may collect tax from rights holders as a subsidy for providing free use to the public. Further, by imposing such a income tax, rights holders may choose to provide their works free of charge in order to be exempted from tax. It has been proved in practice that rights holders can gain more other benefits if they voluntarily renounce their rights and share their knowledge resources. All in all, it is much easier for the public to obtain knowledge through unpaid access to rights holders' authorizations than through fair use.

(3)   Using the income tax from rights holders as a supplement to guarantee free use of protected resources by the public

Countries need to establish a welfare system concerning knowledge resources. Such a system should protect free use by users and at the same time guarantee the benefits of rights holders. For example, many countries have funded the establishment of public libraries and made them open to the public free of charge. At present, due to the increasingly cost of copyright authorization for digital libraries, the cost to get authorization from rights holders is becoming higher and higher for governments. Copyright income tax can be used to establish the digital national libraries, and in turn, the libraries can provide resources to the public free of charge. This is a social welfare that would contribute to the development of science and culture. The part of payment made by the country to obtain authorization from rights holders for the purpose of free use by the public shall be limited to the standard set by the statutory license.

(4)   Improving a subsidy mechanism that encourages innovations

While encouraging the kind of creativity that the creators are not overly influenced by the rights holders and that they try to obtain the works through legal channel, we should set up a subsidy mechanism. Germany, for example, has a subsidy clause in a law issued to help with the development of its domestic film industry. Users can apply for national subsidies to pay for their innovations. Once the work is successful commercially, there should be a mechanism to return the corresponding subsidy to the country.

At present, China has already established certain incentive subsidy policies for innovation, such as the publication subsidy projects in a variety of provinces and cities, the national publication fund projects, etc.. The National Publication Fund was established in 2007 and has been running for more than 10 years. Through the publishing houses, this Fund has facilitated the digital dissemination of a number of books, and particularly the books that have an impact on the development of science education. However, currently, this type of fund mainly focuses on assisting publication, and there is no subsidy for disseminating the published works. Within the framework of statutory license, works related to public interest, such as education, scientific and technological development, should be subsidized so as to help promote the development of science education.

References

1. Lord Denning. Landmarks in the Law [M]. Liu Yongan, Zhang Hong, Trans. Beijing: Law Press, 2000
2. Cooter, Robert D. The Rule of State Law Versus the Rule-of-Law State: Economic Analysis of the Legal Foundations of Development [R]. The Paper for the Annual Bank Conference on Development Economics, Washington, D.C.: World Bank, 1996
3. Basu, Kaushik (2001), The Role of Norms and Law in Economics: An Essay on Political Economy Working Paper, Department of Economics, Cornell University
4. Zhang Jin, Lu Liang. Analyzing Cases of Fair Use [M]. Wu Handong. Intellectual Property Rights Annual Journal (2008) . Beijing: Peking University Press, 2009
5. Jorge Reinbert, Silke von Lewinski. The WIPO Treaties on Copyright [M]. Wan Yong, Xiang Jing, Trans. Beijing: China Renmin University Press, 2008:33
6. Zheng Chengsi. Copyright Law (I) [M]. Beijing: China Renmin University Press, 1990:8
7. Elizabeth Eisenstein. The printing press as an agent of change: communications and cultural transformations in early-modern Europe [M].He Daokuan, trans. Beijing: Peking University Press, 2010
8. Joseph R. Dominick. The Dynamics of Mass Communication: Media in the Digital Age [M], the 7th Edition, translated by Cai Qi, Beijing: Renmin University Press, 2009:19
9. Yu Jiuchang. Instrumentalism of Intellectual Property Rights: Reading Drahos "A Philosophy of Intellectual Property" [M]//Liu Chuntian. Chinese Intellectual Property Review: Volume 1. Beijing: The Commercial Press, 2002:385
10. John Hartley. Creative Industries [M]. Cao Shule, BaoJiannv, Li Hui, Trans. Beijing: Tsinghua University Press, 2007
11. Song Le. Research on Copyright Issues of Internet Snapshot Services [M]//Zhang Ping. Internet Law Review. Beijing: Peking University Press, 2009: 33
12. Xue Hong. Intellectual Property in the Network Age [M]. Beijing: Law Press, 2000: 206
13. Wang Qian. Beyond the "Red Flag Standard": Comment on the First Case of Internet and TV Copyright Infringement [J]. China Copyright, 2011, 6

References 105

14. Song Tinghui. An Analysis of the Legislative Development of "Three-strikes Law" in the World [J]. Intellectual Property, 2010, 20 (116)
15. Li Yongming, Cao Xinglong. Comparative Analysis of Works' Statutory Licensing Systems in Chinese and American Laws [J]. Journal of Zhejiang University: Humanities and Social Sciences Edition, 2005 (4)
16. Hu Kaizhong. A Comparative Analysis of Intellectual Property Law [M]. Beijing: Chinese People's Public Security University Press, 2004: 162

Chapter 6
Improvement of Copyright Collective Management System in Statutory License

6.1 Concept of Copyright Collective Management System

The essence of the collective management organization (CMO) of copyright is that a large number of rights holders choose whether or not to join, or even choose to join different organizations based on autonomy of will according to the agreement made by CMOs.

Copyright collective management is an n important way for copyright to realize economic benefits. Under the copyright collective management system, copyright holders can entrust an organization to uniformly exercise copyright when objectively, they cannot obtain benefits from use of their work by others. The system was first established in 1777 in France by Beaumarchais, a dramatist. The organization was originally named the French Theatre Author and Composers Association. Copyright is a private right. The copyright collective management system has similarities with the trust relationship, and is a special system for managing property. In the copyright collective management system, the copyrights holder entrusts the CMO to exercise his right to the work, and the CMO exercises the right of the work in the name of the copyright holder. This social group is essentially a non-profit organization.

From the date when Ernest Bourges, a French composer wins a lawsuit against the Paris Café in 1847 for the public use of its music as the background music, the copyright collective management system began to be widely adopted in countries around the world. In other words the applying of copyright collective management to the use of background music in public places can be seen as the source and foundation of the legal system of copyright collective management.[1]

With the growing of the public's demand on cultural products and the popularity of digital network technology, the use of a large quantity of works occur. At the same time, the increase in the number of creators and the frequent and widespread circulation of copyrights also complicate and decentralize the ownership of copyright.

---

[1] Amendments to the "*Copyright Law*" (Second draft of the revised draft) of Music Copyright Society of China [EB/OL]. http://www.mcsc.com.cn/informationSociety.php?partid=13&pid=1038.

© Intellectual Property Publishing House 2021
S. Liu, *Rights Limitation in Digital Age*,
https://doi.org/10.1007/978-981-16-4380-4_6

Under such circumstances, it is difficult for the user of the work to quickly and accurately locate the rights holders of the work that he or she needs to use. Even if the rights holders can be identified, it is difficult to negotiate and sign a license agreement with them due to the large quantity of works to be used. Excessively high transaction costs make it difficult to achieve effective connection and cooperation between users and rights holders, and users are in an awkward situation of "either not use or infringement". Social media organizations such as radio and television organizations and websites are faced with a fiercely competitive market environment and a wave of changes in technology and business models. It is no longer feasible for them to stick to the old rules. They must be integrated into the flood of unauthorized use of works. under such circumstances, copyright and its related rights (hereinafter referred to as "copyright") are difficult to obtain effective protection, the users of the works faces enormous legal risks, and the authority of the legal system is undermined.

Establishing a scientific and rational copyright collective management system is an effective measure to solve this problem. By creating an integrated copyright trading platform, the collective management system allows users to efficiently clarify the ownership of works and obtain permission, to avoid the worries of being held legally liable. Meanwhile, the rights holders are enabled to use the information gathering capabilities and negotiation capabilities of CMOs to realize their remuneration right (especially the remuneration right for the overseas use of the work). Further authors are free from the cumbersome licensing issues, and can concentrate on the creation. In short, under such a system, the use of extensive, large-scale, and repeated works no longer need to get the "peer-to-peer" proprietary authorization. This can effectively reduce transaction costs, promote the protection and circulation of copyrights, and take into account the interests of rights holders, users, and the public. To a large extent, the operational effect of the collective management system shows the level of development of a national copyright legal system.

The copyright collective management system, as a system to ensure that rights holders get paid, has played an important role developed so far.

As an intermediary organization that exists in the transaction process between the copyrights holder and the user, the CMO will inevitably generate corresponding social costs. When parties of a transaction are able to complete the market transaction on their own, the supply and demand relationship is sufficient to induce the parties to find a value point of market equilibrium. Under such a circumstance, the rights holder is in a position to set the price and prohibition right is applied. As a third party in the transaction process, the existence of the CMO of copyright does not affect the above-mentioned transactions completely determined by market. Its role is mainly reflected in the following three aspects:

Firstly, "When external economic factors of benefiting third parties other than the parties, caused by adopting this system, are generated, such use behavior will not only be widely recognized, but also generate necessity of a claim for compensation

6.1 Concept of Copyright Collective Management System

to ensure the excitation of development of results".[2] Article 23 of the amendment to the Copyright Law of China in 2001 has such provisions.[3]

Secondly, it can avoid the failure of transaction due to the high transaction price set by the rights holder taking advantage of his monopoly position resulted from the prohibition right.

Thirdly, it can avoid the restrictions on the freedom of personal use brought by the absolute prohibition right. As such restrictions objectively reduce the resources available for innovation, and harm the core value of the intellectual property system to encourage innovation.

---

[2] Tamura [1].

[3] Article 33 of Copyright Law of Japan: (1) It shall be permissible to reproduce in school textbooks ("school textbooks" means textbooks authorized by the Minister of Education and Science or those compiled under the authorship of the Ministry of Education and Science to be used for the education of children or pupils in primary schools, junior high schools, compulsory education schools or senior high schools or other similar schools; the same shall apply hereinafter) works already made public, to the extent deemed necessary for the purpose of school education. (2) A person who makes such reproduction shall inform the author thereof and pay to the copyright owner compensation, the amount of which is fixed each year by the Commissioner of the Agency for Cultural Affairs, by taking into account the purpose of the provision of the preceding paragraph, the nature and the purpose of the work, the ordinary rate of royalty, and other conditions. (3) The Commissioner of the Agency for Cultural Affairs shall announce in the Official Gazette the amount of compensation fixed in accordance with the provision of the preceding paragraph. (4) The provisions of the preceding three paragraphs shall apply mutatis mutandis with respect to the reproduction of works in textbooks intended for correspondence courses of senior high school education (including the latter stage of high school education) and in guidance books of school textbooks intended for teachers (these guidance books shall be limited to those published by the same publisher of the textbooks).

Article 46 of Act on Copyright and Related Rights (German): (1) Reproduction, distribution and making works available to the public shall be permissible after publication where limited parts of works, of small-scale literary works and of musical works, individual artistic works or individual photographs are incorporated in a collection which combines the works of a considerable number of authors and is intended, by its nature, exclusively for use during religious ceremonies. The purpose for which the collection is to be used shall be clearly stated on the copies or when making them available to the public. (2) (repealed); (3) Work on reproducing the work or making the work available to the public may only begin after the intention to exercise the entitlement pursuant to subsection (1) has been communicated by registered letter to the author or, if his place of residence or whereabouts are unknown, the holder of the exclusive right of use and two weeks have elapsed since the letter was sent. If the place of residence or whereabouts of the holder of the exclusive right of use are also not known, notification may be effected by publication in the Federal Gazette. (4) The author shall be paid equitable remuneration for the exploitation permissible in accordance with this provision. (5) The author may forbid the exploitation permissible in accordance with this provision if the work no longer reflects his conviction and he can therefore no longer be reasonably expected to agree to the exploitation of the work and he has for that reason revoked any existing right of use (section 42). The provisions under section 136 (1) and (2) shall apply accordingly.

6.2 Status Quo of China's Copyright Collective Management System

No field of the intellectual property system in China can get rid of the shadow of the government's top-down method in its designing of system. The establishment of the CMO in copyright cannot be established solely relying on the autonomy of the rights holder. The National Copyright Administration strictly controls the establishment of the CMO. It has a dominant intervention power over the internal regulations of the CMO, and may even intervene in the consideration for the use of works. This is related to the foreign origin of China's intellectual property system. In order to adapt to international treaties, for many years before the establishment of the association, the National Copyright Administration has required that without its authorization, no unit or individual should engage in collective copyright management activities. That is, record company and individuals with the copyright on musical works are prohibited to jointly protect the economic interests of the copyrights holders. Such administrative measures seem to be made in accordance with the provisions of the current laws of our country. But in fact, such a legislative idea is precisely a negation of the "private right nature of copyright", which is the most basic property of copyright. The law has granted the government excessive power, and the legal system is formulated in an improper way. This makes the law a real evil law for copyrights holders. By recognizing the legitimacy of the copyright CMO through the approval of the administrative act, the copyrights holders are prohibited from realizing their copyright interests in various ways. Any non-profit organization is the result of voluntary association of citizens. The state administrative organs should respect citizens' constitutional rights of association. The current China is in a period of social transformation and is undergoing a process of transitioning from a government-led society to a pluralistic order based on socially spontaneous organizations. When the copyright law is to be amended again, the copyright CMO should be clearly written into the copyright law, and the identification of the legal status of the organization should have a transition from administrative approval system to the registration system.

Facing serious problems of poor copyright authorization mechanism and trading rules in China at present, the construction of the copyright collective management system is particularly important. At present, China has established five copyright CMOs for different types of works. Music Copyright Society of China, established on December 17, 1992, is currently the only music copyright CMO in China, with an aim to safeguard the legitimate rights and interests of composers, lyricists and other music copyrights holders. China Audio-Video Copyright Association, which was established on May 28, 2008, is the only audio-video CMO in China, implements collective management of the copyright of audiovisual programs and the rights related to copyright. China Written Works Copyright Society, which was established on October 24, 2008, is a non-profit social organization engaging in copyright services, protection and management for the purpose of safeguarding the legitimate rights and interests of copyrights holders, and is the only CMO for copyrights of written works in China. China Film Copyright Association is a non-profit social organization with

6.2 Status Quo of China's Copyright Collective Management System

legal person qualifications that is legally engaged in the production and operation of film production in China, and is the only copyright CMO of the rights holders of Chinese film works. The predecessor of China Film Copyright Association was China Film Copyright Protection Association established in August 2005. In July 2009, China Film Copyright Protection Association was transformed from an industrial rights protection organization to a copyright CMO. It was officially renamed China Film Copyright Association in October 2009. Founded on November 21, 2008, Images Copyright Society of China is a copyright CMO jointly established by China Photographers Association, a number of photography groups and more than 100 famous photographers, and is the only corporate legal person institution engaged in images copyrights collective management in China.

Since the establishment of these copyright CMOs, they has played an important and positive role in promoting the protection of copyright and the dissemination and use of works. However, they still need to be upgraded in terms of business models, management practices, and professional talents. Because China's CMOs had been established for a short period of time and lack sufficient operational experience. Rights holders and users have insufficient understanding and biases on the nature and role of CMOs, and the public's awareness of intellectual property rights is relatively weak. Thus, China's copyright CMOs face prominent problems such as limited number of members, lack of representativeness, low recognition, and having difficulty in charging royalties.

6.2.1 Extended Collective Management System

The newly added "extended collective management system" in the third draft amendments to the *Copyright Law* has become a hot issue for all related sectors of the society. The first draft amendment adds the provision for the extended collective management of copyright. This amendment is questioned by many rights holders as it makes rights holders impossible to claim damages from those who have paid royalties to CMOs through litigation. The second draft amendments still retains the relevant provisions of extended collective management, but limits the scope of application of extended collective management and refines and supplements the regulatory rules for CMOs. This change reflects the trend of "strengthening rights exclusiveness and reducing rights restrictions". However, the legal and industrial circles still have doubts over the extension of the collective management system. Some people think that the rights of CMOs can only be derived from the authorization of rights holders, and "legal provisions" on circumstances should not be increased. Because the copyright is a private right, whether or not the CMO can be authorized should be decided by the rights holders, not directly prescribed by law.

In fact, it is not created by China to have the law stipulate the rights that CMOs can manage. Many countries in the world have already established such a system.

112   6 Improvement of Copyright Collective Management System ...

The EU Directives on Copyright and Neighboring Rights relating to satellite broadcasting and cable broadcasting stipulates that cable broadcasting adopt the compulsory collective management system, while wireless broadcasting adopts the extended collective management system. The German Collective Management Organization Law stipulates that if the rights holder fails to transfer the cable broadcasting rights stipulated in the first sentence of the first paragraph of Article 20 of the Copyright Law to the CMO, the CMO shall be deemed to have the right to manage the right. Article 217-2 of French Intellectual Property Laws tipulates that "from the date of the entry into force of No. 97-283 Law on March 27, 1997, the right for that the performances of performers, recording products, and video products which have been teleported from members of the European Community are wired, synchronized, completed, and broadcasted without change as stipulated in this law, is only exercised by a remuneration collection and distribution association." Article 144A of *Copyright Law of the United Kingdom* stipulates that: (1) This article applies to text, drama, musical or artistic works, recording products, and film copyrights holders granting or refusing to authorize another European economic area country to cable and retransmit the radio broadcast containing its work, this right is hereinafter referred to as "wired retransmission rights." (2) The wired retransmission rights can only be claimed by the authorized institution to cable operators. (3) If the copyrights holder fails to transfer its cable retransmission rights to an authorized institution, an authorized institution that manages the same type of rights shall be deemed to have been entrusted to manage his rights. Article 180 of the Italian Copyright Law stipulates that: ① The exclusive right to be broadcast by cable can only be exercised by the copyrights holder and copyrights holders through the Italian Association of Authors and Publishers. The Italian authors and publisher associations exercise the rights of copyrights holders in relation to the rights of performers and performer relief groups or other collective management organizations established to manage related rights. ② The above-mentioned management organization may also provide services to rights holders who are not members but belong to the field of the organization in accordance with the same standards as other members. It can be seen that the extended collective management system has sufficient legislative basis.

This author believes that extended collective management is a way to simplify the traditional collective management model, and is a modern mechanism to ensure that rights holders can better manage their rights. It can effectively remove the original sin of the user and reward the rights holders in a fair manner. However, it should also be noted that the effective operation of the mechanism depends on the support of a mature rule of law environment and related supporting mechanisms, and the application of the mechanism has strict conditions.[4] Therefore, before the legislator makes a decision, it is still necessary to further examine how the countries or

---

[4] For example, UK Copyright and the Right of Performer "Extended Collective License" 2014 regulations impose stricter restrictions on the application of extended collective management: extended collective licenses implement strict application approval systems; and stipulates for a wider range of extensible licenses; the collective license organization must permit others to use according to the provisions of the extended license scheme, and may not transfer the approval obtained; the approval of the extended collective license may be revoked by the minister of state; the copyrights holder has

6.2 Status Quo of China's Copyright Collective Management System

regions that have adopted the extended collective management mechanism limit the applicable conditions and scope of the mechanism, what corresponding safeguard measures are made for the operation of the mechanism, and how is the actual operation effect. After that, they toned to estimate the necessity and feasibility, and cost and benefit of establishing an extended collective management mechanism taking into consideration China's realities and needs in the field of copyright protection and circulation.

Take musical works as an example, the use of musical works presents the characteristics of a large number of rights holders, dispersed rights, relatively concentrated users, large quantity of use, and wide use. Market practice has proved that the rights such as broadcasting rights, performance rights and information network communication rights of musical works can be realized through the copyright collective management system. According to the statistics of the 2014 Annual Report of the International Confederation of Societies of Authors and Composers (CISAC),[5] 87% of the 7.8 billion Euros of work usage fees charged by the global copyright CMO for various users belong to the usage fee of musical works This also verifies the special value of the copyright collective management system in the protection and use of music works. It is worth noting that China's CMOs have explored a set of operating models of "package license plus tort liability debt guarantee" in response to the difficulties in confirming right, authorization, and charging in social media's use of music works in a large quantity. This model roughly means that the CMO signs a "package agreement" with the broadcast and television organizations and internet companies that are the consumers of musical works, and the user pays the royalties for all the musical works he used to the CMO. The CMO transfers the usage fee to the copyrights holder (whether or not it is a member) based on the use report of the musical work. If the rights holder who is not a member claims damages to the user and causes the user to bear legal responsibility, the CMO provides guarantee for the debts that the user should bears.[6] The essence of this mode of operation is to carry out the "extended management" by agreements, and thus can effectively reduce the high legal risks faced by the social media due to the difficulty of obtaining the authorization of the massive music works they use. Further, as CMOs have stronger negotiation ability and information acquisition ability than the copyrights holder or the copyright agency company, they can better protect the rights of the rights holder. It is necessary for legislators to pay attention to the "native rules" spontaneously

---

the right to withdraw from the extended collective license, exclude or limit the grant of licenses; extended collective licenses can only be non-exclusive licenses.

[5] Quoted from the 2014 Annual Report of the International Confederation of Societies of Authors and Composers (CISAC).

[6] Since September 2010, Music Copyright Society of China has signed a "package" payment agreement with China Central Television, China National Radio and China Radio International, and more than 30 provincial TV stations in China. At present, according to a "package" model, Music Copyright Society of China further expand the use fee collection business for national local radio and television organizations. At the same time, Music Copyright Society of China is gradually establishing a "package" agreement-based music payment model with the well-known mainstream internet enterprises in China.

114   6 Improvement of Copyright Collective Management System …

formed in such a market practice, and examine the actual utility of the operating model, the positive and negative attitudes of the stakeholders, the legal status of the parties and the legal nature of their actions, in order to provide local experience for the design of copyright collective management system.

6.2.2 Royalty Rates

Will the rights holder abuse his absolute status when he is able to replace the middleman, who monopolizes the market? This author believes that this problem can be solved by free market competition. With the popularity of digital communication at present, the law should pay attention to the issue of rates and compensation in statutory licensing. Taking the copyright collective management system as an example, according to the provisions of the "Regulation on the Collective Administration of Copyright" in China, the copyright CMO itself formulates relevant licensing standards, and the copyright management department of the State Council publicizes the above standards. Each copyright CMO would set special charging standards (including rates and units of calculation) for fields which have a relatively concentrated demand for reasonable licensed uses. In the calculation unit of reasonable royalties, the general literary works are calculated in the counts of words, musical works in pieces, length of use and area of a space, the works of art and photography in frames, and poems in lines. However, industry associations can set their own specific charging standards (including rates and calculation units) for fields that have a relatively concentrated level of demand for some reasonable licensed uses. Judging from the current data, although the royalties charged by China's copyright CMO has shown a trend of continuous growth year by year, compared with the volume and activity level of China's cultural industry, there is still room for improvement in the execution capability and efficiency of the licensing standards.

In UK, copyright CMOs have the right to establish licensing standards in the industry. Such standards are enforced after being published somewhere, and have mandatory effects. Meanwhile, the unit value of copyrights is also measured mainly by economic methods during the formulation of licensing standards. Moreover, various relatively easy-to-operate license rates and calculation units are set according to the characteristics of the business scope. Unlike China, UK adopts a more scientific and meticulous method in the formulation of licensing standards. For example, regarding the units used in the calculation of royalties for musical works, the British copyright CMO does not use numbers as a unit in practice as this requires the support of reliable data. Its calculation is based on location. For instance, British Phonographic Performance Ltd. (PPL), one of the world's most powerful copyright CMOs, collects up to 170.8 million pounds of royalties for copyrights holders every year. It has over 10,000 members who are copyrights holders and accept over 300 new members each month. This is mainly because, on the one hand, PPL has a strong and comprehensive copyright database; on the other hand, PPL caters to the needs and habits of consumers, and focuses on balancing the interests of all parties in

6.2 Status Quo of China's Copyright Collective Management System

setting licensing standards. PPL sets the licensing standard based on the consumer's usage requirements, and further divides the different usage requirements to form different royalties. Such a set of procedures, which can be used repeatedly, can automatically generate royalties and complete the payment process in most cases only by providing information online. This greatly facilitates the consumers in fulfilling their license requirements. Meanwhile transparent and clear licensing standards also make consumers easily anticipate their cost to be licensed, and make rights holders foresee their acquirable benefits. As both parties can carry out the external supervision of copyright collective management while enjoying convenience of the collective management of copyright, this guarantees the healthy and smooth operation of the copyright collective management system.

In judicial practice in China, it is believed that the purpose of infringement of copyright litigation is not to resolve disputes related to licensing rates or licensing standards. However, in calculating the amount of damages resulted from infringement, it will refer to the existing licensing standards of copyright CMOs. Therefore, by analyzing the current calculation method of the amount of infringement damages in our courts, we can see the shortcomings of China's license standards in copyright collective management, and find useful reference for the establishment and improvement of the standards.

In China, we should pay attention to the balance of interests and procedural fairness in the process of making licensing standards, and establish supervision and relief rules in the formulation process. If rules are not established based on the competing of related interest groups, the fairness of such rules is questionable. Therefore, during the formulating of the licensing standards, it is important to solicit the opinions of the licensees. Only when the license standards are agreed by the parties can it be implemented. If the copyright CMO and the licensee representatives cannot agree on the license standards, the license standards cannot be implemented. Once the formulation process is deadlocked, it will have an adverse impact on the interests of all parties and the healthy development of the industry. Therefore, it is very important to establish a fair procedure and supervision and relief rules in the process of formulation. The relevant government departments need to supervise and provide guidance over the problem. Supervision can both guarantee fairness and impartiality in the formulation of licensing standards, and the smooth implementation of licensing standards.

Reference

1. Yoshiyuki Tamura. Intellectual Property Law of Japan [M]. Zhou Chao, Li Yufeng, and Li Xitong, Trans. Beijing: Intellectual Property Publishing House, 2011: 21

Chapter 7
Code Is Law

7.1 Digital Technology Reshaping Economic Behavior

In 2015, Imogen Heap, Grammy Award winner and British female singer and song-writer, sold her MP3-format music works to users by directly using the e-wallet to receive the digital currency Ethereum using blockchain technology. She made a qualitative distinction of the use behavior and set corresponding prices. For individual consumers, whether they are listening online or permanently downloading, they only need to pay a small amount of money; while for commercial use of the works, the price of a musical work is much higher than the price for an individual.[1] Thanks to this smart contract mechanism, rights holders no longer have to sign separate license agreements for commercial use of works. Heap believes that the music industry needs change, and the use of blockchain technology will change the landscape of the music industry and help creators maximize their profits.[2]

As the commercial subject of market transactions, whether it is a business or an individual, its economic behavior is usually conducted after cost accounting. Economic behaviors in the network environment are broader and more diverse. In this transaction-friendly environment, individuals can easily play different roles in production, promotion, and sales, and independently perform multiple functions in the value chain. Just like Heap mentioned above, when rights holders can complete

---

Lawrence Lessig, professor of Stanford University, mentioned this point of view: the code of conduct in cyberspace is built together by laws, social norms, markets and codes. Code-based software or protocols determine people's way of using the Internet. Code is the cornerstone of the internet system, which has the ability to regulate individual behavior through technical means.

[1] UjoMusic, established in the UK in 2015, provides musicians with a platform to publish and manage their ownmusical works to achieve music copyright management, revenue and automatic distribution of income through technical support. Imogen Heap posted its single "Tiny Human" on this platform, which costs $0.60 for downloading the product, $0.006 for online listening, and $1500 for commercial use.

[2] WIPO Conference on Global Digital Content Market [EB/OL]. (2016-04-20) [2018-05-30]. http://www.wipo.int/meetings/zh/2016/global_digital_conference.html.

© Intellectual Property Publishing House 2021
S. Liu, *Rights Limitation in Digital Age*,
https://doi.org/10.1007/978-981-16-4380-4_7

the transaction on their own and can maximize the return from the circulation and use of their musical works without any intermediaries, they will tightly hold all rights in their hands. This gives the rights holders a more aggressive role in decision-making and bargaining, and makes them a party with absolute monopoly. This new code of conduct is a new set of values formed in the interaction between law and technology.

Internet technology is gradually forming a monopoly model from the initial free and decentralized model. Technology pioneers always begin to explore new technical directions from the perspective of respecting human rights, and their starting point may be respect for personal privacy, or may be to respect and protect people's basic right for acquiring knowledge. The Internet has also nourished the pirated industry in an environment advocating "anonymity" and "freedom". Nowadays, technology is fixing the many problems that it brings about, including piracy, with its own updates. However, legal means should also be relied on to protect the interests of all parties. In the future, the blockchain technology may need to be relied on to achieve honesty on the Internet.

Blockchain technology is a new application model of computer technology, which is born out of the underlying technology of bit network operation. It is essentially a database with the following core features: decentralization, trustless, collective maintenance, reliable database, timestamp, and asymmetric cryptography, etc.

Decentralization can make everyone an independent entity that does not rely on any intermediary or platform, giving people an opportunity to complete transactions only based on a string of characters in their own computer. Trustless means that the completion of a transaction does not require endorsement by a trusted credit agency, and that trust relationships between transaction parties are a kind of consensus reached between the participating parties before choosing this transaction mode, which becomes a mechanism. Collective maintenance is a way to maintain the normal operation of the blockchain, which require participating of all nodes in the network under the concepts of "majority rule" and "everyone is born equal". Reliable database is designed by blockchain technology; it is the unchangeable transaction information that corresponds each transaction with the occurrence time of the transaction enabled by the introduction of time stamp. Asymmetric cryptography specifically refers to a rule design or algorithm to realize the normal operation of the blockchain. Time stamp which cannot be tampered can solve the problem of data tracking and information security. The secure trust mechanism solves the problem of lack of trust.

In view of the development of Internet technology in recent decades, knowledge has always been the first object of development and prosperity in the network economy, and intellectual property is more naturally applicable to digital circulation, with copyright as the core of communication. Furthermore, the complexity of the use of music work and the issue of rewards to the rights holders under the impact of technology always exists. Therefore, the development and maturity of blockchain technology will have a profound impact on the transformation of the entire music

7.1 Digital Technology Reshaping Economic Behavior

industry.[3] The features of blockchain technology will be the best solution to market failure in the musical industry resulted from the distribution of interests.

7.2 Distributed Storage Protecting Rights

The traditional network storage system usually saves data on a storage server in a centralized way. Today, the business service model of cloud storage has become very common, the major feature of which is that storage is service. With the program provided by the storage service provider, users can save their data by directly uploading their data to the cloud. However, this model has security risks as it makes users lose absolute control of their data.[4]

(1) Content being controllable

Digital assets can be completely controlled by computer after blockchainization of storage, without the need for human factors under existing technology. Everyone can have their own exclusive key to encrypt their digital assets, which can fundamentally solve data theft and privacy issues. For the consumers, what they can do is to abandon the traditional ways to acquire rights to works and popular platforms and turn to new approaches or choose among different platforms. But for artists, they can fundamentally change the previous state of control over their works, set prices on their own, and control the user's use of their works and the payment methods.

(2) Resource sharing

The blockchainization of storage makes it possible to share idle disk resources. The storage design based on the incentive mechanism will encourage users with idle storage resources to provide services to the storage network without having to gain the trust of other users. This greatly reduces the cost of storage services and saves social resources, and is essentially a concept and practice of sharing economy, that is, reuse of idle resources through the internet platform. Moreover, encryption measures can avoid obtaining of personal data resources by providers of storage servers, thus greatly reducing the possibility of piracy. Thus server providers no longer need systems such as the safe harbor principle.

(3) Infringement being traceable

Enabled by the time stamp technology, blockchain realizes the function that account books can't be falsified. Meanwhile, each transaction record can be traced back and publicly available, which is undoubtedly "excavating a tomb for the pirated

---

[3] Olusegun Ogundeji. Blockchain Going for a Song: New Tech Tunes Up Music Industry [EB/OL]. [2016-05-22]. https://cointelegraph.com/news/blockchain-going-for-a-song-new-tech-tunes-up-music-industry.

[4] Fu et al. [1].

users to expose the infringement and consolidate the evidence of infringement". Therefore, literally, the blockchain technology has brought about a "thiefless world", and operation rules of the blockchain directly replace the functions of law.

7.3 Smart Contracts Guaranteeing Fair Trade

Many countries have amended their laws due to the impact of digital technology. However, in practice, copyright transactions involve many links and the whole system is very complicated. Although new technologies have created new forms of works, and have brought about new behavior and lifestyle, many rights holders do not get their share of returns despite the high sales figure. The development of information technology has accelerated the changes of many industries, reshaped the business model, reconstructed the way of distributing benefits. During this process, the law has never stopped adjusting itself to the changes. Especially for those transactions that are chaotic, complicated, trivial and small in transition amount, a simple and efficient mechanism is needed. To solve this problem, digital technology is currently the best solution. Before amendments are made to the law that lags behind, the smart contract in the blockchain technology environment directly provides a mechanism to ensure the smooth completion of the transaction.

The concept of a smart contract was originally proposed by scholar Nick Szabo. It refers to "a set of promises defined in digital form, including agreements on which contract participants can implement these commitments.",[5] namely, a computer protocol which completes the exchange, verification or fulfillment of the agreement through informatization. Its most important feature is that it can be completed automatically without relying on the endorsement of a trusted third party, and cannot be repented. While the data is being encrypted, it can be controlled by blockchain codes such as smart contracts. Different from the traditional internet technology, the blockchain technology is capable of making rules by itself and implementing rules automatically. The current blockchain technology can use technical methods to implement contract principles and solve the problem of trust. Besides completing the transaction, it also reflects the consensus of the community, establishes a trust relationship, and realizes the rights and obligations of both transaction parties.

The object of a smart contract is the data resources stored in the blockchain. The rights holder can formulate its own charging rules for a certain digital asset, and decide different participants and profit distribution for each transfer of right to use. These operations are conducted using smart contracts, and are witnessed and decentralized by network storage distributed throughout the world, with transaction records being recorded on the blockchain in a blockchain way. By utilizing characteristics that blockchain transaction records are open and transparent, and cannot be tampered, it not only clarifies the ownership of assets, realizes the transfer of digital assets and the transfer of use rights through blockchain accounting, and eliminates the possibility of

---

[5] Bocek [2].

piracy of digital assets. Each person has a unique encryption key for each of his own digital assets based on the code system of the blockchain account. When ownership or use rights are transferred, the encryption method for the data is a double encryption of both ownership encryption by data owners and use right encryption by data users. Even if the data is cached locally and propagated to others, the user only has access to encrypted data asset after paying the consideration to the asset owner.

7.4 Conclusions

Every minor adjustment of the legal system may be a process of fixing technical bugs in order to rebalance the distribution of interests between rights holders and the public. However, the conflict of interests brought by technology will eventually need to be solved through the advancement of technology itself. While the process of amending the lawn usually takes a long time, the iteration of technology itself always surprises us and easily solves the difficult problems in the "old world". Therefore, in the modern society where economic growth is based on technological development, the legal system should respect technological development. In the framework of the intellectual property system especially, the law should respect the balance between private rights and public interests in system design. By restricting the boundary of fair use, expanding the scope of statutory licenses, and improving the copyright collective management, the law will present a more majestic face to deter those illegal acts in today's Internet based economic environment. Blockchain technology will technically support rights holders to monopolize their work in an unprecedented way. This author believes that the widespread use of this technology is an inevitable trend. At the same time, the study on the rights limitation system will become more and more important with the raising of the monopoly status of rights holders in order to ensure the interests of users.

In many developed countries, the evolution of society, economy and culture is a smooth process. But in China, this is a vast change, although this change has taken us for nearly 100 years. The old Copyright Law in China which is "Triggered by the Guns", is now shifting to a conscious law driven by domestic economic development. In this process, both legislation and judicial practice have experienced countless ups and downs, and criticisms. The reorientation of Copyright Law in China will not only affect the interests of thousands of rights holders and the public, but also readjust the balance of interests. It will play an immeasurable role in the development of traditional culture and ideology in China. The historical responsibility of the legislators is to choose a value orientation, to determine the status of this law in the history of social development, and to ensure that it can adapt to the rapid changes in technology in the next 5–10 years.

References

1. Fu Yingxun, Luo Shengmei, Shu Jiwu. Survey of Secure Cloud Storage System and Key Technologies [J]. Computer Research and Development, 2013 (50)
2. Thomas Bocek. Digital Market places Unleashed [M]. Springer-Verlag GmbH, 2017:169–184

Printed in the United States
by Baker & Taylor Publisher Services